Here's a collection of how-to's, practical ideas, resources and detailed instructions for implementing a churchtime program for children in grades 1-6. In most churches, churchtime means the session following Sunday School when parents are in the adult worship service. Other churches use these ideas on Sunday evening or during the week. If your church already has a churchtime or weekday ministry for children, this book is filled with ideas to help you strengthen it.

If you've ever wondered—
- What does it take to have a successful churchtime ministry for children?
- How do I start churchtime in my church?
- How do I recruit and train a staff for a churchtime program?
- How can I keep children interested in Bible learning and worship?
- How can parents be involved in a churchtime program?
- How does churchtime relate to Sunday School?

... then this book is for you!

First Church of the Brethren
1340 Forge Road
Carlisle, Pennsylvania 17013

CHURCHTIME for CHILDREN

By Jim Larson

Developing a Successful
Churchtime Ministry for
Children in Elementary Grades

A Division of G/L Publications
Glendale, California, U.S.A.

I especially want to thank
Georgia Ana Larson, Sheryl Haystead
and Shirley Mize for their valued assistance
in developing this handbook.

Scripture quotations used in this book are from the:
New International Version, New Testament.
Copyright © 1973 by New York Bible Society International. Used by permission.

Published by Regal Books Division, G/L Publications
Glendale, California 91209
Printed in U.S.A.

ISBN 0-8307-0561-9
Library of Congress Catalog Card No. 77-92692.

CONTENTS

PREFACE

In churches of all sizes around the world, people are ministering to children. In addition to Sunday School, churches have devised programs for churchtime, on Sunday mornings or evenings or on weekdays.

The purpose of this handbook is to provide guidelines for children's ministries which supplement but are different from that of the Sunday School. You can expect to gain from this book a better understanding of ministry with children plus helpful skills for conducting an effective churchtime program.

Each chapter concludes with two special features:

In Case You're Wondering ... provides answers to typical questions people ask about the subject of the chapter.

Check Yourself ... provides questions for discussion, reflection or further study.

May God guide your understanding of an effective ministry with children, as you enable children to learn God's Word and share His love with them.

Jim Larson

PART I

GETTING STARTED

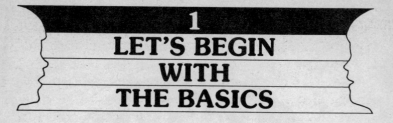

1
LET'S BEGIN
WITH
THE BASICS

Joel arrived at church with a special gleam in his eye. "Mrs. Hansen," he said to his teacher, "my mommy had a baby yesterday!" Joel's teacher listened with genuine interest as Joel shared that happy news ...

When Heather arrived, she looked sad. She walked slowly and talked in a whisper. Her teacher, Mr. McArthur, found out that her grandmother was very sick. Together they prayed for Heather's grandmother ...

If God has called you to be a co-worker with Him in the lives of the children, you're someone very special. Maybe you work in a churchtime ministry on Sunday mornings or evenings or in a weekday program for children. Whatever your ministry role, your work with children can be vital and significant.

You're an important person to God—so important

that He sent His Son to die in your place! Each child to whom you minister is also of great importance to Him. God is aware of every effort you make to reach each one for His sake.

You're important to your church—so important that its children are entrusted to your guidance. You are a "vital link" in the church's overall ministry to people as you reach out to their children in Christian love, sharing the good news of the gospel with them, and nurturing them as Christians.

You're important to the children, too! They may not always tell you, but in their way children appreciate the time you spend with them and the attention you give them. You're an important person—to God, to the church, and to the children.

The Bible contains many important guidelines which can help us have the best ministry possible with our children. Let's look at some "action words" that describe what God wants us to do in our ministry with children.

BIBLICAL GUIDELINES
FOR MINISTRY WITH CHILDREN
1. Teach

Even back in Old Testament times, God directed His people to teach their children spiritual truths. God's people were to teach their children wherever they were (see Deut. 6:6-9).

This directive is also clearly stated by the apostle Paul: "We have put our hope in the living God, who is the Savior of all men, and especially of those who believe. *Command and teach these things*" (1 Tim. 4:10, 11, italics added). In teaching children, we have opportunity to guide them to a *personal*, life-changing knowledge of their heavenly Father.

11

What is it that God wants us to teach? He wants us to teach others about His love as demonstrated by the life, death and resurrection of Jesus Christ. Paul describes our message in this way: "We are therefore Christ's ambassadors, as though God were making his appeal through us" (2 Cor. 5:20).

God wants us to introduce children to Jesus Christ and provide opportunity for them to believe in Him as their Saviour and Lord. And that's not all! We have the privilege—and responsibility—of guiding children toward spiritual maturity, the lifelong process of becoming Christlike.

God wants us to be His representatives to children—to model His love to them. The Bible tells us to teach children about God wherever we are, at church or in our homes, in more formal teaching/learning situations, on outings, or in visits with the children in other informal settings (see Deut. 6:6,7).

Remember that a teacher of children does not have to have great Bible knowledge or be a person without problems. But a teacher needs to study God's Word and sharpen his or her teaching skills to do the best possible job of sharing the Word with children effectively.

2. Lead

The person who ministers to children is not only a teacher, he is also a leader. God's Word describes our leadership role in this way: "Be shepherds of God's flock that is under your care, serving as overseers—not because you must, but because you are willing, as God wants you to be; not greedy for money, but eager to serve; not lording it over those entrusted to you, but being examples to the flock" (1 Pet. 5:2,3).

The leader of children is concerned about their total welfare—physical, emotional, social, intellectual, as

12

well as spiritual needs. He takes the initiative in finding ways to meet the needs of the children to whom he ministers.

For instance, Miss Walker began bringing a light breakfast for her class when she discovered that several of the children did not eat breakfast before coming. Their attentiveness greatly increased!

And a department leader named Mr. Dreyer stood at the door to greet new children and involved them in an activity they especially enjoyed.

A children's leader does not have to feel that he or she always has to have "instant" answers for every question a child asks. Rather, the leader guides the child to discover what God's Word says about specific concerns the child has expressed.

The leader of children is not a "policeman" seeking to make every child "sit still and listen" while he teaches, nor is he merely a glorified baby-sitter who keeps children from tearing a room apart. But the leader of children is a committed Christian who lovingly guides children to an understanding of God's Word, spending time and effort to make the learning enjoyable and profitable.

3. Model

"Stop talking! What you're doing is speaking so loudly I can't hear a word you're saying!"

It's true. Children learn more from what they observe adults doing than they learn from what is said.

God's Word tells us to be an example to the children to whom we minister, an example in "speech, in life, in love, in faith and in purity" (1 Tim. 4:12).

Now, that's hard work! It's far more difficult to be a living example of God's love than it is to merely talk about it. For instance, if a person talks about loving other people but speaks with a tight-lipped, angry expression on his face or in his tone of voice, a child will remember these angry feelings rather than the words about Christian love.

Children learn a truth more thoroughly and put it into practice more frequently when they can observe someone doing it. For instance, children respond more generously when they can observe someone performing a generous act, than when they only hear someone talk about the need to be generous.

If all our actions speak this loudly, we need to ask ourselves:

• As we talk with children about God's love, are we being loving in our relationships to them and to other adults working with us in the program?

• When we talk about being truthful, are we genuine and honest with the children?

• When we talk about patience, are we patient with the children as we interact with them?

• As we encourage the children to share their concerns with the Lord, do we also pray with them about our own difficulties—as may be appropriate?

It's not always easy to do what we say, is it? But if we want our ministry with children to be effective, we need to be aware of the importance of being consistent examples of the truths we communicate.

4. Serve

The person who ministers to children is also a servant who eagerly seeks to meet the needs of children, even when personal sacrifice of time or money becomes necessary.

Jesus' disciples had difficulty understanding how to be servants. They even argued over who was the most important disciple. Jesus responded by telling them,

"Whoever wants to become great among you must be your servant, and whoever wants to be first must be your slave—just as the Son of Man did not come to be served, but to serve, and to give his life a ransom for many" (Matt. 20:26-28).

Adults should be involved in a children's program to serve the children, to lovingly meet children's needs and to help them discover how Christ loves them (see 1 John 3:16). A true servant is more concerned about the welfare of those he serves than about his own needs. In teaching children, we need to do everything we can to provide Bible learning experiences that help each child sense that he or she is wholly accepted and loved by God.

5. Love

God wants us to love children! The Bible says, "Let us not love with words or tongue but with actions and in truth" (1 John 3:18).

God's Word also provides a very specific, helpful guide for determining the quality of our love. The apostle Paul describes love in this way: "Love is patient, love is kind. It does not envy, it does not boast, it is not proud. It is not rude, it is not self-seeking, it is not easily angered, it keeps no record of wrongs. Love does not delight in evil but rejoices in the truth. It always protects, always trusts, always hopes, always perseveres" (1 Cor. 13:4-7).

It is not always easy to love like that when working with children. We may not feel patient or kind when a child has just been insulting or rude. We may not always find it easy to forgive and forget, but may be tempted to hold grudges or show preferential treatment to children who are easier to love than others. But God wants us to love others, just as He has loved us. (See Appendix A for specific suggestions for ministering to children.)

6. Pray

None of this is possible—teaching, leading, being an example, serving or loving—without God's help. The apostle Paul really knew what he was talking about when he said, "Pray continually" (1 Thess. 5:17).

The leader of children needs to take this advice to heart. Think regularly about the special needs of each child. Pray for the insight that will enable you to meet these needs.

Pray for patience and love, especially for those children who may be special "behavior challenges." (Never call a child a "problem." A behavior problem may be something he has; it is not something he is.) Every child is known and loved by God. But some children may be greater challenges than others because of their behavior or other needs.

The Bible also tells us to pray for each other—to pray for the other members of the leadership team—that there may be a spirit of unity and love (see Jas. 5:16). Pray that God will continue to work in each adult's life, guiding each leader, teacher and parent to be open to learning in their own lives.

God WANTS us to talk with Him, to share our concerns with Him. He has promised not only to listen to us, but to answer our prayers. The answer may not always be a YES; maybe it will be a NO or a WAIT. But God will answer our prayers (see Matt. 7:7-11).

If we are growing in our relationship with God, we have a strength and insight at our disposal not available to us when we work entirely on our own.

7. Plan

God wants us to use the abilities we have and the

resources available to us to provide the best possible ministry for children. This cannot happen without careful planning and organizing in regular consultation with other leaders in your program. (Chapter 9 provides guidelines for planning.)

Think carefully about what your children need, what your goals are, and how you plan to reach these goals.

FINALLY ...

Do you see now why you are such an important person as a minister to children? God's Word says you are to teach, serve, be an example, love, and pray for the children with whom you have contact. And God wants you to plan carefully so that you are an effective minister in His name.

No matter how inadequate you may feel about the task God has called you to do, remember that it is GOD who calls you to work with children. He has promised to help you do the best possible job with each child.

Make the prayer of Hebrews 13:20 your prayer as you prepare for your ministry with children: "May the God of peace, who through the blood of the eternal covenant brought back from the dead our Lord Jesus, that great Shepherd of the sheep, equip you with everything good for doing his will, and may he work in us what is pleasing to him, through Jesus Christ, to whom be glory for ever and ever. Amen."

IN CASE YOU'RE WONDERING ...

1. *What are some ways that I am an example to the children in my program?*

Children seem to have "X-ray" perception when it comes to observing what we do and hearing what we say. Most children can "see" right through a person who says one thing and does another.

We are examples to children in many ways including:
- Being prepared
- Being on time
- Treating other leaders with love and concern
- Learning names
- Encouraging rather than criticizing
- Listening, not just talking.

Remember that your example of loving actions and words will not only be observed by the children. Your example will be imitated!

2. How can I adequately show concern for the children when I'm the only leader with 20 children?

There's no easy answer to this one. Admittedly, it is difficult to show personal attention to more than a few children at a time. Getting additional staff help is essential for your situation. (See chapter 9 for recruiting helps.)

But while you still have a large group, consider the following suggestions:

- Keep a roster of children who attend. Go over the names during the week to become familiar with them.

- As children arrive, locate yourself so that you can personally greet by name as many children as possible. Make a point of learning each child's name to personalize your greeting and make him feel welcome.

- Assign simple responsibilities to older children, who can serve as student aides and help keep things running smoothly.

- Use learning activities which children can work on independently.

- Take every opportunity to chat briefly with the children. Phrases such as, "Good work!" "I'm glad you're here!" and "I'll be praying for you this week" (and be honest about this!) are ways to show concern for children.

• Greet children by name when you see them around the church campus or at other times.

See Appendix B for additional suggestions for ministering to children.

CHECK YOURSELF

1. List two or three specific ways a leader of children can teach, lead, be a model for, serve and love them.

2. Think of someone who helped you by example to understand a truth. For example, what person has helped you by example to understand the word "love"?

3. As you reflect on the action words ("lead," "love," "model," etc.) discussed in this chapter, which of these do you find the hardest to do? You may want to share this need with a Christian friend who will pray with you and for your ministry with children.

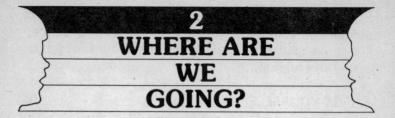

2
WHERE ARE WE GOING?

CHURCH IS MORE THAN SUNDAY SCHOOL!

Looking back now as adults who grew up in the church, many of us recall our weekly hour in Sunday School as among the most valuable Bible study experiences in the church. Even so, this was but a very brief time for learning even the most basic Bible truths. In many churches today, Sunday School is still limited to an hour a week. No matter how effectively the Bible is taught in the 52 hours a year of Sunday School, guiding children in the church toward spiritual maturity need not be restricted to these few hours.

Increasingly churches are discovering ways to expand their Christian education ministry to children by including extended session or churchtime, Sunday morning, evening or weekday ministries. During these additional

20

informal Bible learning times with the children, much can be done to supplement and enrich Sunday School learning experiences. In addition to being a valuable supplement to Sunday School for most children, a churchtime ministry may be the only contact some children who do not attend Sunday School may have with Christian people and the teachings of Scripture.

GOALS OF SUPPLEMENTAL CHILDREN'S MINISTRIES

There are several general goals to guide you in planning an extended or supplemental churchtime or weekday ministry with children. No matter when you schedule this kind of ministry in your church, aim to help each child have the opportunity:

1. To become a member of God's family.

A primary goal of any ministry for children is a clear presentation of how to become a Christian. A simple, biblical non-pressured presentation of the gospel, with opportunities for children to receive individual counseling, should be an essential feature of any children's ministry. (See Appendix C for suggestions.) Often through the conversation and example of Christians and the teaching of God's Word, the Holy Spirit works to bring a child into the family of God by faith in the Lord Jesus Christ.

2. To understand biblical principles for Christian living and practice them in life-related experiences at church and at home.

Children need patient guidance in understanding how to live as Christians. A supplementary churchtime or weekday program needs to provide a variety of informal opportunities for adults and children to talk together concerning what God's Word says about living the Christian life in everyday ways. Children also need opportunities to actually practice these biblical principles,

21

by sharing and discussion, roleplay, or other Bible-related activities.

The key to Christian growth is not only to KNOW what God's Word says about living as a Christian, but to actually OBEY God's Word. A vital ministry to children needs to provide opportunities for this kind of growth to take place.

3. *To participate with God's family in worship and praise to God.*

Worshiping God together can be one of the great joys for members of God's family. Worship in a children's ministry should be carefully designed to meet the needs and level of children's understanding. Since most children are energetic by nature, their worship experiences need to be informal and allow for movement and involvement. Children readily become restless and uninterested when an adult style of worship is used.

Children profit from participating in worship experiences that have been carefully planned to honor the Lord as well as to be enjoyable for the children. This investment in careful planning can pay off in later years, when children may participate meaningfully in worship as young people and adults.

4. *To develop nurturing relationships with members of God's family—adults and peers at church and at home.*

Church needs to be a happy place for children to be, and meaningful relationships with Christians are an important part of a happy church experience. An elementary-age child can be strongly influenced not only by his parents but also by other adults. What better place for children to have adult examples and friends than among Christians in their church!

Adult contacts at church can reinforce the Christian values and experiences a child may already have in his home. Where there is no Christian influence in the home, adult friends of children at church play an even more important role.

Elementary-age children are learning to develop friendships with their peers, and these relationships also have a powerful influence on the values, attitudes and behavior of children. For this reason, children need frequent contact with peers who are members of God's family.

Children learn a great deal from the example and values of those around them. A Christian education ministry to children needs to provide opportunities for observing and developing relationships with adults and peers which are both nurturing and satisfying. (See Appendix B for additional ideas for building relationships with children.)

5. *To understand and participate in ways God's family is at work in the world.*

Children are action-oriented. Most children would rather get involved and do something than sit still and talk about an idea. Children need not only to be aware of what Christians are doing in the world, but to actually become a part of God's work. Children respond positively to learning about Christians involved in ministries at home and around the world. To actually participate in some realistic service or missionary project is even more exciting!

6. *To enjoy and appreciate relaxed times of fellowship.*

Children need relaxed times of informal, large muscle activities, particularly if they have just completed an hour of Sunday School or a day of school.

Playing simple games and enjoying nourishing refreshments together often are natural settings for informal conversation with children. Significant conversation often takes place during these less structured moments. As children enjoy refreshments, for example, adults can chat informally with individual children about their interests and activities.

Leaders whose planning takes into account the needs and interests of children usually find that children respond with genuine enthusiasm and appreciation.

ONE OTHER THOUGHT ...

We have described in this chapter some goals you can adapt for your children's ministry. And as you plan, remember to make the children the focus of your planning. Some questions to discuss are: How can we plan to meet the needs of the children by our churchtime ministry? What activities can we include that children enjoy? What do the children already know about God? How do we build on that knowledge? Do their homes provide any enrichments or any problems to which we need to be sensitive? How can we accomplish the six goals which have been described?

Looking at your churchtime program through the eyes of children will greatly strengthen your ministry. The tendency is to let adult needs and abilities or the limitations of facility, budget and staff determine goals for a children's ministry. Commit yourself before God to tailor-make an effective children's ministry, to meet their specific needs for growing as God's children.

IN CASE YOU'RE WONDERING ...

1. I understand what you're saying about the goals of children's ministry which is supplemental to Sunday School. But what are the overall goals for a children's ministry?

Good question! See Appendix A at the end of this book for some help.

2. Why do we emphasize the need for children having positive experiences at church?

That's another important question! At a very young age children gain impressions and begin to form attitudes based on their experiences with people and places. Even as babies in the church nursery, if their experiences are positive, they can develop the feeling that church is a good place to be, and that the people there are good to be with.

The child who does not find friends or is bored by what he finds at church will probably drop out of church during the later elementary or junior high years. Such negative attitudes about the people and programs of the church are difficult to change!

Let's do some "preventive" work and be sure that children have an experience which is both enjoyable and nourishing!

Subsequent chapters in this book will give you more details on schedules, organization, and activities for children.

3. In a churchtime program, why not have just a worship service?

Worship is an essential part of such a program, of course. But let's remember that children need movement and opportunities for creative activity. So, by interspersing group times of praise with Bible learning activities which require movement and individual involvement, you can meet needs essential for building children's interest and eagerness to learn.

CHECK YOURSELF

1. Use the following chart to evaluate how well your present program is meeting the six goals described in this chapter for a churchtime ministry. Then plan specific ways to improve your children's ministry.

GOAL	LEVEL OF ACCOMPLISHMENT	STRENGTHS/ WEAKNESSES
List each of the six goals described in this chapter.	How does your children's ministry accomplish this goal? If this goal has not been implemented in your program, list in the space below specific ways in which it can be accomplished.	Strengths and/ or weaknesses of this approach to meeting this particular goal.
1. 2. 3. 4. 5. 6.		

2. Have the parents of one of your children tape informal interviews with children who are now participating in your children's ministry. (The children may not be as frank with you as they would with someone who is not involved in your program.) The children should be asked: What do you like most about (use the name of your program here)? What do you like least? Then, at a leaders' planning session, play the taped interviews and discuss what you hear. What insights do the children give you concerning your ministry?

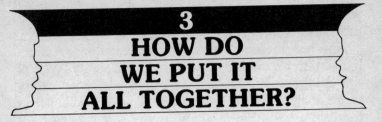

3
HOW DO WE PUT IT ALL TOGETHER?

Thorough planning of your churchtime ministry to children is of great importance. A children's churchtime program that runs smoothly is no accident. Personnel, facilities, and the potential enrollment will all be factors to consider as you organize your program. In this chapter, we will deal with the questions of grouping and grading, as well as schedules.

ORGANIZING YOUR CHURCHTIME PROGRAM

In order to effectively accomplish the goals discussed in chapter 2, limit the size of your department to approximately 30 children, with a total staff of four—the leader, teachers, parent helpers, and/or aides. When a department gets much larger than 30 children, the staff tends to spend more time handling organizational matters and problem situations than focusing attention on individual children. If your program grows to include more than 30 children, plan how you can divide the group into two departments meeting in separate rooms, with a leader and a teacher who will build their departmental staff as attendance increases.

Another important factor in implementing an effective children's ministry is the grade and ability levels of the children. The broader the span of age or ability levels of children in one department, the more challenge the leader will have in adapting the activities to meet such varying abilities and interests.

For example, children in grades 1 and 2 work well together in one department. If the number of children is less than 20, grade 3 children could also be included. Programs involving children of a wide age range tend to focus on the middle ages; thus the needs of the younger and the older children are often not met.

Maybe you're wondering how to have more than one departmental program if only one room has been made available.

Consider these options:

• Explore all church facilities. Could you exchange some rooms with other age groups meeting at the same time?

• Could you divide a larger area? Could walls be added or removed to accommodate this kind of change without affecting other groups? Could portable walls be purchased or constructed to use your space more efficiently?

In most situations, the best plan is to have each group of children use the same room for both Sunday School and churchtime. The question of how to provide adequate staff for this plan will be discussed in chapter 9.

GROUPING THE CHILDREN
In planning the grade levels and sizes for your program, keep in mind the needs of your children and how they learn best.

In any children's program, there is value for children to learn in a variety of group sizes. Large groups (including everyone in the department) are vital for building enthusiasm and group spirit. In a large group, a leader can communicate with the whole department of 30 children together.

Children also need personal attention from adults with whom needs, joys and questions can be shared. Personal conversation with a child makes him feel accepted and an important part of the group. Such individualized conversation is not often appropriate in the large group.

In a small group the adult has frequent and natural opportunities to guide the conversation toward the unit theme. Most children are apt to participate in a small group of 6-8, where they feel free to express their ideas and concerns and become actively involved in the learning process.

SCHEDULES

In planning your program, remember to include a variety of activities to meet the interests and needs of the children. The four basic plans on the following page have provided the needed variety and worked well in many different kinds of church facilities. (NOTE: Chapters 4-7 provide a description of these activities.)

IN CASE YOU'RE WONDERING . . .

1. For what age children should we provide churchtime?

As you deal with this question, it is important to determine what you want children to learn and experience. Your facilities and style of corporate worship may also influence your decision. It is generally agreed that children in at least grades 1-3 benefit more from an

SCHEDULE SUGGESTIONS

BASIC PLAN (for a 60–95 minute program)

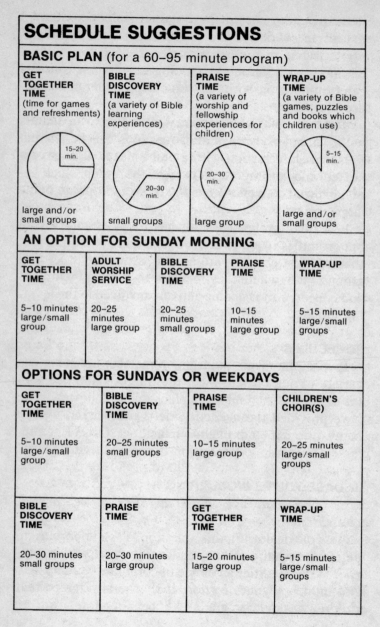

GET TOGETHER TIME (time for games and refreshments)	BIBLE DISCOVERY TIME (a variety of Bible learning experiences)	PRAISE TIME (a variety of worship and fellowship experiences for children)	WRAP-UP TIME (a variety of Bible games, puzzles and books which children use)
15–20 min.	20–30 min.	20–30 min.	5–15 min.
large and/or small groups	small groups	large group	large and/or small groups

AN OPTION FOR SUNDAY MORNING

GET TOGETHER TIME	ADULT WORSHIP SERVICE	BIBLE DISCOVERY TIME	PRAISE TIME	WRAP-UP TIME
5–10 minutes large/small group	20–25 minutes large group	20–25 minutes small groups	10–15 minutes large group	5–15 minutes large/small groups

OPTIONS FOR SUNDAYS OR WEEKDAYS

GET TOGETHER TIME	BIBLE DISCOVERY TIME	PRAISE TIME	CHILDREN'S CHOIR(S)
5–10 minutes large/small group	20–25 minutes small groups	10–15 minutes large group	20–25 minutes large/small groups

BIBLE DISCOVERY TIME	PRAISE TIME	GET TOGETHER TIME	WRAP-UP TIME
20–30 minutes small groups	20–30 minutes large group	15–20 minutes large group	5–15 minutes large/small groups

effective Sunday churchtime program than from attendance in an adult service—particularly after a 60-90 minute period in Sunday School.

2. *What can older elementary-age children (grades 4-6) do during church if we only provide a churchtime program for younger children?*

Parents of older children may want them to participate with their families in the adult worship services. In such instances, the pastor will plan features of the worship to be of interest to older children.

In some cases, you may find that older children may be able to assist you as aides in your churchtime program. Others may simply enjoy being participants. Meet with parents to discuss available options.

3. *We have children's choir rehearsal as part of the churchtime hour. What can I do with children who just don't like to sing?*

If there are children who do not enjoy the children's choir program, evaluate the choir program to discover possible reasons. Are children expected to sit for a long time? Are the words of the songs understandable to children? Are the melodies happy and enjoyable for children to sing?

Some children enjoy participating with a choir if they can provide accompaniment with rhythm instruments, piano, autoharp, guitar and drums. Most children, if provided with these options, will want to be in the choir.

Ask those who still don't want to participate to assist one adult by preparing materials for next week's program. Or provide books, puzzles, etc., for these children to use.

4. *Our children participate in the first part of the adult worship service before they leave for churchtime. What are some ideas for involving the children in the adult worship service?*

If children are present during any part of the adult worship services, suggest to your pastor that he plan during that portion of the worship service to include a hymn understandable to children. The pastor's explanation of unfamiliar words, and the main thought behind a hymn, are important worship aids for children. Some pastors also include an object lesson and Scripture for children. Asking one family each week to be involved in the worship service (singing, sharing, reading Scripture, etc.) could be helpful.

Another idea is to provide a sheet for children to write or draw answers to one or two questions related to the sermon or worship theme. These sheets are then collected by ushers (as children are dismissed to churchtime) and are given to the pastor. His reading or showing a sheet completed by a child the previous week can be encouraging to children and of much interest to the congregation.

5. *When should children be expected to participate in the adult worship service?*

An older elementary-age child is beginning to understand many abstract concepts and can begin to participate with understanding in an adult worship service. So when the older children are expected to attend adult worship services with their families, be sure that their needs and interests are considered by those planning your church's worship experiences.

CHECK YOURSELF

1. List the advantages of each department group having no more than 30 children. What should be done when a group gets larger than 30?

2. Which of the schedule plans will best fit your church's needs?

PART II

A PLAN FOR CHURCHTIME

4
GET TOGETHER TIME

Now that you have established goals and guidelines for a children's ministry, and have considered grouping, scheduling and organization, what do you do once the children have arrived?

Every church is unique, with different staff, children, groupings of children and program format. Some churches have a churchtime or extended session on Sunday mornings to supplement their Sunday School ministry. Other churches have a Sunday evening or weekday ministry.

No matter when your program is held, four basic components need to be included: Get Together Time, Bible Discovery Time, Praise Time and Wrap-Up Time. Chapters 4-7 will describe each of these basic program elements and why they are essential.

Get Together Time is the first segment of your program and should last 15-20 minutes. This time helps the children feel welcome and provides activities to get "the wiggles" out in preparation for Bible learning and Praise Time.

NOTE: If two or more Sunday School departments have been combined for your program, Get Together Time may be done in separate Sunday School rooms, with everyone coming together for Bible Discovery Time.

A WARM WELCOME

The children are arriving now for your program, and each one needs to know you and the other teachers care for him. Greet children personally with a "Hello, Tina," or a "Hi, Bobby. I'm glad you're here today." Every child needs to be recognized as an individual who is worth knowing and appreciating.

Learn names. Notice new clothes, haircuts, bandages and changes in normal moods. Listen attentively as children share what has happened to them during the previous week. Affirm the children with your kind words, letting each one know how special he is to you.

The friendly, welcoming atmosphere you and your staff create helps children feel secure and loved and open to respond positively to your program.

PHYSICAL MOVEMENT

Children need to move around and stretch their muscles. An informal activity time will meet this physical need and give the children an opportunity to enjoy being with one another. Children who have been sitting quietly in Sunday School need a change of pace and a chance to exercise large muscles. In school, children have recess in mid-morning to provide for such activity.

Games, action songs that call for bending, stretching or jumping and supervised nature walks in the area of your church are ways you can provide for physical movement. Children arriving for a weekday program also profit from such activity, especially if they have been in school all day. (See Appendix D for additional information.)

You will find that children can be more attentive and interested if they first have this opportunity for physical movement. As teachers participate with the children in these informal activities there are additional benefits in terms of building relationships.

Begin games as the first two or three children arrive. Generally, Get Together Time is conducted in a large group, although from time to time you may want to consider having several small group activities simultaneously for variety.

Here are some sample game ideas:[1]

1. Fast Pass: Players sit in a circle. Teacher begins playing a song on record player or tape recorder. When the music begins, players pass the ball around the circle from one person to the next as fast as they can. When the music stops, whoever is caught holding the ball is out. The last person left in the circle wins.

2. Knock the Can: Divide the players into groups of five of six. The groups hold hands to form a circle. Place in the center of each circle two tin cans, one on top of the other. The players try to make each other knock over the cans. When a player knocks over the cans, he must sit out until there is one player left, and the game begins again.

3. Blow Ball: Mark a start and finish line with chalk or masking tape on the floor. Players line up along the start line. Give each player a ball (use Ping Pong balls or cotton balls). The players must blow the ball along the floor from the start line to the finish line without touching the ball. The first player whose ball crosses the finish line wins.

REFRESHMENTS

Children also need physical nourishment. If this program is part of a Sunday morning ministry, serve light refreshments to the children during Get Together Time. If this program is conducted on a Sunday night or weekday, you may want to serve the refreshments at the conclusion of the program.

Children enjoy nourishing refreshments such as crackers and cheese, peanut butter on celery, fresh fruit, carrot strips, flavored yogurt, and fruit juice. Parents and children enjoy working together to prepare and serve the snacks.

Be sure to provide opportunity for children to use the washroom facilities.

IN CASE YOU'RE WONDERING ...

1. What can we do during Get Together Time if we have a limited facility for such activities?

If your facility is quite limited, consider taking the children for a nature walk if weather permits. Guide children to observe God's creation. Also, select activities (such as small group games or those which do not involve running) which require less space.

2. How do I handle the transition from Get Together Time to the next segment of the program?

Develop a recognizable signal (a bell, musical chord, timer, etc.) that tells everyone that a new activity is beginning. Teachers and aides need to be aware of the time schedule and guide children in activities so they are ready to leave when the signal sounds. An advance warning that time is nearly up will allow children to conclude an activity without a frustrating rush.

CHECK YOURSELF

1. List two reasons why giving a warm welcome to children is important for a successful churchtime ministry.

2. Identify three needs of children which can be met through the activities of Get Together Time.

---

1. An extensive list of suggestions is provided in "Living in God's Family," Gospel Light's churchtime curriculum kit for children.

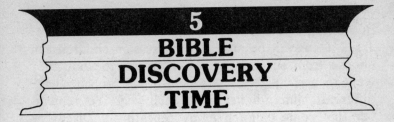

5
BIBLE DISCOVERY TIME

After spending 15-20 minutes in Get Together Time, the children move into Bible Discovery Time. Bible Discovery groups, each composed of 6-8 children and a teacher or aide, allow opportunity for children to discover and explore Bible truths through creative learning activities, such as art, drama, or music.

ORGANIZING BIBLE DISCOVERY TIME

Each teacher or aide is responsible for a Bible Discovery group. Approximately 6 to 8 children will be in each Bible Discovery group. Thus, for a program of 30 children, at least four activities should be provided.

During each session of a unit, teachers guide the same Discovery group activity but with different children participating at each session. For example, in each session of Unit 1, Mrs. Smith guides the Bible Discovery group in viewing and discussing a filmstrip about the life of Jesus. However, because at each session children can choose from several Discovery groups the one they want to participate in, Mrs. Smith will probably have different children in her group each week. Yet remember that some children enjoy repeating a Discovery group.

The time for children to choose their Bible Discovery groups can take place by assembling the whole group at the beginning of Bible Discovery Time. A teacher briefly describes each of the activities and guides the children to make their selections. Another way to let children choose is to provide sign-up posters during Get Together Time.

BENEFITS OF BIBLE DISCOVERY TIME

Children need new experiences. They are curious and ready to learn. A child develops as he is challenged to try new things, is encouraged to explore and grow, and is affirmed for each new effort to learn. Bible Discovery groups provide ways to help children grow in understanding of God's Word.

Bible Discovery groups provide a variety of active Bible learning experiences built around God's Word for the children. In these informal learning groups, children can discover what an enjoyable experience exploring and applying the Scriptures can be. And appropriate adult encouragement will help each child feel successful.

BUILDING RELATIONSHIPS

These small-group activities also provide opportunity for relationships to develop between the children and the teachers. In small groups, interaction between teacher and child can be more personalized and meet the special needs and interests of each child.

Bible Discovery groups provide a natural setting for the children to enjoy each other. Here, children can try out new behaviors you are encouraging them to develop. For example, in a unit on sharing, encourage children to share supplies, written activity instructions, etc.

As you work with the children, compliment them whenever you can. Children appreciate personal attention! Always be quick to comment on good behavior or thoughtful deeds. Not every child will be attractive or have new clothes, but every child can do kind deeds, show consideration for others, or assume responsibility. There is always something each child does well for which you can commend him.

Praise children who are generous and loving toward other children. For example, say, "Johnny, I like the way you shared the crayons with Suzie." Encourage them to share their needs with both the children and teachers in your program. The Bible Discovery groups can be just the place to meet the need children have to relate to adults and other children.

When children enjoy experiences at church, they feel that the "church" is a happy place to be, with people who appreciate and help each other.

PROVIDING CHOICES

Children who may choose between two or more activities are usually more motivated to learn than those who have no choice and are expected to be involved in something of little interest. For example, you can increase children's desire to learn about Abraham, by providing more than one way for them to do it. Let them choose whether they will illustrate scenes from the life of Abraham. Or, plan a simple drama so children can act out a scene from Abraham's life.

BIBLE LEARNING THROUGH ACTIVITIES

In Bible Discovery groups, children can discover Bible truths and relate the Bible content to their everyday lives. Such activities as art, drama, writing, music, listening posts and research will encourage children to study God's Word for themselves.

Sometimes, the Bible truths may be expressed in a story the children hear on cassette. Sometimes, the children read the Scriptures to discover the truths for themselves. A filmstrip can also be used to present a Bible truth. Whatever media is involved, the teacher is the key to guiding the children through conversation and activities to understand these Bible truths. The teacher can also use unit-related Bible verses in conversation while guiding the activities.

Allowing children opportunities for creative expression has other benefits. Rarely is lack of interest or boredom a problem where teachers have carefully planned such experiences. When children are expected to sit still for an unreasonable length of time or when a program is predictable and boring, problems are more likely to occur.

Here are some specific examples of what children enjoy doing during Bible Discovery group time to respond to Bible truths.[1]

Art

Children glue pictures to sides of a box to make a box mural of the story of the seven days of creation, for example.

Dough art or clay are fun to use for making Bible figures and faces showing what the persons might have felt.

Wet chalk adds greater luster for drawing pictures; or dip colored construction paper in water and use chalk to draw on the wet paper to illustrate God's creation.

Drama
Individuals or small groups pantomime a key Bible verse or truth, or act out a Bible story for a "Who Am I?" game. For example, children could act out the story of Paul's conversion.

Children relate a Bible verse to everyday life situations by completing an open-ended story.

Written Communication
Children write sentence descriptions of selected pictures. (Leader records the descriptions young children may give orally.) For example, such pictures could illustrate examples of what God has created.

Provide a large picture of a tree, with Bible or life-related questions written on the trunk. Children can write answers on leaf-shaped pieces of paper and attach these "leaves" to tree branches.

Oral Communication
Children complete an open-ended life-related or Bible story pre-recorded by leader on cassette.

Children listen to brief Bible story, and then retell the story from the point-of-view of one of the five senses. For example, "What would you have seen if you had been in this situation?" or "What would you have heard if you had been there?"

Music
Children make a song chart by replacing some words of a song with pictures on a large sheet of butcher paper or poster board.

Puppets can be used for teaching children words and motions to a song.

Children complete open-ended songs. Examples: "How Do You Show Love for the Lord?" and "How Does Jesus Show He Loves Me?" (See *Sing to the Lord* songbook for children.)

Research/Listening Centers

Children listen to a Bible story on cassette tape, or view it on filmstrip or film. An art activity may then be used to provide for learner response.

Have children look at an illustrated Bible story or life-related pictures and talk about what they see happening in the pictures.

Bible Games

Children can make a Bible game using a familiar game such as Tic-Tac-Toe and writing theme-related questions and answers.

The leader might provide a Bible game for children to play. (See *Creative Bible Learning for Children: Grades 1-6* for suggestions.)

PROVIDING INSTRUCTIONS

Providing clear written or recorded instructions can help children work independently of your direct supervision in the Bible Discovery activities. If materials are accessible and simple to use, children will find it easy to follow the instructions you have given on a tape recorder or poster.

It is important to develop gradually a child's ability to function independently. Begin by giving a child one simple task to complete. If he accomplishes the task successfully, then increase the complexity of your instructions. Generally, an elementary-age child can follow two to five steps in completing an independent activity.

IN CASE YOU'RE WONDERING ...

1. How are Bible Discovery groups different from a Sunday School class?

Children usually do not work for more than one session in a Bible Discovery group, while each child is usually assigned to meet in the same Sunday School class for a quarter or a year. Membership of Discovery groups changes each week, while the leader remains the same for each session of the unit. The leaders each prepare for one learning activity per unit, since they repeat their activity each week of the unit with different children involved.

In a Sunday School class, a teacher often tells a Bible story. In a Bible Discovery group, the teacher will more often guide the children to discover Bible truths for themselves.

2. How can I adapt Discovery group activities to allow for variations in reading and writing skills among the children?

As you plan activities, include an alternative to the skills of reading or writing. For instance, provide instructions on tape, ask an older child to read instructions to a nonreader, or use symbols and pictures to replace as many words as possible in instruction copy.

Children who have difficulty writing may often be able to express their thoughts by drawing, or by dictating what they want to say to a leader or aide. Remember too, that if children are given the opportunity to choose which Discovery group they will participate in, they will probably choose activities which involve skills they have mastered.

NOTE: For help in dealing with children who are hyperactive, shy or aggressive, see Appendix D.

3. What can I do if I don't have enough teachers and aides to provide more than one or two activities?

Your goal should always be to maintain the ratio of one teacher or leader for every 6-8 children. However, if you are shorthanded one week, or are just beginning to recruit your staff, here are some suggestions: Involve older children in helping younger children. Choose one activity that the entire group can complete. Keep table groups small and move among them. An activity with instructions clearly written on a poster will allow you to converse personally with some children while others are working. By decreasing the amount of time you must spend giving instructions and distributing supplies, you can increase the amount of interaction you have with individuals. Also, consider having a quiet alternative (books, puzzles, records, etc.) available for children who finish early.

4. *What are some good words and phrases to use in praising, recognizing and encouraging children as you work in Bible Discovery activities?*

Good question! Here are some examples:

"That's very good, (child's name)." "Much better."

"Thank you, (child's name)." "Good work!"

"This really pleases me." "That's right!"

"I like the way you're working." "Terrific idea . . ."

"You have good ideas." "Good job . . ."

"Thanks for your help." "Super!"

"Let's show the others what you've done." "Good thinking." "Keep it up."

"I like the way that you . . ." "How interesting!"

"Now you've got it!" "Exactly right."

"Thank you for . . ." "What neat work."

5. *Will more than one Bible Discovery group in the same room be distracting?*

Children easily adjust to several activities happening in the same room. If an activity is interesting to them, their focus will be on what they are doing.

CHECK YOURSELF

1. List some additional art activities to use during the Bible Discovery group time.

2. List reasons why child and teacher need small group interaction.

---

1. Complete plans are provided in "Living in God's Family," Gospel Light's churchtime curriculum kit for children.

6

PRAISE TIME

Children need informal worship and fellowship opportunities at their own level of understanding. Such experiences need to be designed so that children can express their love and praise to God. Children may express praise to God at various times and places, formally or informally, individually or in a group—whenever they think upon God's great goodness, His power and love.

Praise Time can provide informal opportunities for worship, as well as for getting acquainted, discussing Bible truths and life-related concerns.

PARTS OF PRAISE TIME

When planning worship opportunities for children of elementary grades, arrange a variety of opportunities for praise within a 20-30 minute period. While some children will respond through music, others' responses may not be audible or visible, but will be expressed silently within their own minds and hearts as the Holy Spirit brings the truth of a Scripture portion into focus and meaning. For this reason, plan Praise Times carefully to provide a variety of experiences so that there will be opportunities for response by each of the children with whom you work.

Each Praise Time in the "Living in God's Family" churchtime curriculum is built upon a four-week unit theme and includes a variety of experiences such as Bible stories and verses, songs and rhythms, Bible games, puppet conversations, Bible dramatizations, interviews, and many other experiences related to the unit aim.

Helping children learn how to talk with God can be one of the most rewarding aspects of your ministry. Encourage the children to respond with phrases to complete a sentence like: "Dear God, we thank you for ..." or "Dear God, please help me ...." Use prayer songs as another way of guiding children to pray.

Easily made puppet characters can be used to introduce a song, ask questions about a Bible story, or to discuss or act out a real-life situation related to the unit theme. Using puppets is a proven method for capturing children's attention and guiding their responses.

Occasionally, invite people with artistic, musical or some other special ability to be included as "special features" at Praise Time. Children profit by becoming acquainted with a variety of Christian youth and adults. Use these people to teach a new song, sing a musical selection, or briefly share ways God has helped them.

A SAMPLE PRAISE TIME PLAN

To summarize the elements we have been discussing for Praise Time, the following is a sample of what may be included in a meaningful and effective churchtime period of praise and fellowship. This particular Praise Time is part of a get-acquainted unit used at the beginning of the school year.

Materials needed: • Bible • Red, yellow, blue and green construction paper squares (4x4 inches, 10x10 cm) • Matthew Puppet • *Ethel Barrett Tells Favorite Bible Stories, New Testament* record[1] • *Sing to the Lord* songbook[1] and *Children Sing to the Lord* record[1] • Picture of people in early church eating, praying and talking together • Butcher paper on which you have lettered words to chorus of "We Are the Church" • One small bean bag • Word chart for "Happy, Happy" • Puppet stage • Four cardboard boxes—one labeled "RED," one "GREEN," one "YELLOW" and one "BLUE."

Preparation: 1. Follow instructions and patterns in *Learning Resources[1]* to make Matthew Puppet (a young boy).

2. Make Interview Cards by printing these sentences on construction paper squares: RED: I feel really happy when ... My favorite TV program is ... YELLOW: After school I ... I really get angry when ... BLUE: I really like to play ... I have trouble with ... GREEN: I wish I could ... With my friends I like to ...

3. Optional: Cover Interview Cards with clear adhesive-backed paper to prevent tearing.

4. Use a piano, guitar or autoharp chord, a bell, a timer, or play music from *Children Sing to the Lord* record to signal the beginning of Praise Time. Each week two minutes before Praise Time is to begin, use the same signal.

Song

"Happy, Happy." Begin singing song as first children

50

come to the area designated for Praise Time. Use word chart and record to help children become familiar with the words and melody.

Puppet Script

Matthew begins "walking" around stage, looking lost and worried as teacher is welcoming children.

Teacher 1: I'm glad all of you are here today. Let's see now ...

(Matthew interrupts Teacher 1 by saying feebly, "Help! I need help!" Teacher 1 stops and turns to see what is happening.)

Matthew: (louder voice) Help! I need help! Who can help me?

Teacher 1: Well, hello. What's your name?

Matthew: (quietly) Matthew.

Teacher 1: What was that? I can't hear you. Speak louder.

Matthew: Matthew, sir.

Teacher 1: What's your problem?

Matthew: I'm lost. Can you help me?

Teacher 1: Sure. Where do you want to go?

Matthew: (clearing throat) I-I'm looking for the church. Where is it?

Teacher 1: The church? You're looking at it.

Matthew: (looks around) Where? I don't see a church.

Teacher 1: It's right here!

Matthew: (Head down, discouraged) Oh, you're no help.

I guess I'll just have to keep looking for the church. (walks off stage)

Teacher 1: Poor Matthew. I thought I gave him an answer that would help him. I wish he'd stayed because he'd have found out who the church really is. Oh well,

I'm glad you're all here. We will have a good time together.

Bible Story

Introduce the Bible story with ideas like this: "Listen carefully to this Bible story to find four things the people in the early church did together." Play "The Story Without an End," from *Ethel Barrett Tells Favorite Bible Stories, New Testament* record. Or tell the story of the early church in Acts 2—4. If possible, show Bible picture of these events as you tell story. After Bible story let four volunteers each point out on picture one thing people in the early church did together.

Puppet Script

Teacher 2: This teacher introduces himself (work, family, hobbies, etc.) and begins to introduce other teachers. Matthew is wandering across stage again, looking lost. Teacher 2 notices Matthew.

Teacher 2: Can I help you?

Matthew: I hope so. I-I'm looking for the church.

Teacher 2: You're looking at it!

Matthew: Wha-a-t? I don't see a building that looks like a church.

Teacher 2: Of course not.

Matthew: Then, where's the church?

Teacher 2: Right here!

Matthew: (rather irritated) Oh no! Not again! You're no help either.

Teacher 2: (looking rather puzzled, shrugs shoulders, then continues introducing other teachers and aides. Matthew wanders off stage.)

Getting to Know You

Teacher 2 continues, "To help us get to know each

other, let's play 'Getting to Know You.' We'll play this game often. The person being interviewed throws his bean bag into one of the cardboard boxes. Then he chooses an interview card of the same color as label on box." Choose two or three children to be interviewed by determining whose birthday is closest to today's date. Teacher interviews children (who stand approximately six feet from board when throwing bean bags); then Teacher 2 interviews Teacher 1.

Puppet Script

Matthew: (wandering around stage again)
Teacher 1: Matthew, can we help?
Teacher 2: We really would like to help you.
Matthew: Please! I'm looking for the church. Where is it?
Teacher 1: That's easy. You're looking at it!
Teacher 2: Sure! *I* am the church . . .
Matthew: But . . . you don't have any windows . . . or doors!
Teacher 1: Well, we are the church . . .
Teachers 1 and 2: TOGETHER . . . .
Matthew: You mean—the church is *not* a building?
Teacher 1: RIGHT!
Teacher 2: The church is a *people*—!
Teachers 1 and 2: We are the church together!
Teacher 1: Hey, those words sound familiar.
Teacher 2: Yeah! They're the words to a song.
Teacher 1: Let's sing it together! (Teachers 1 and 2 sing chorus of "We Are the Church.")

Song

"We Are the Church." Use word chart and record as children and Matthew Puppet sing chorus to this song. Repeat two times. After song, Matthew Puppet exits.

Prayer

Teacher 1 thanks God for the church and all the people who are part of it.

A FINAL WORD

One additional point to remember in structuring the Praise Time experience is that children (like adults) want to be needed. So, plan ways children can help teach songs, use puppets, provide special music, read Scriptures, participate in Bible games or moments of prayer. Tell the children you appreciate their assistance.

IN CASE YOU'RE WONDERING . . .

1. How can I guide children in worshipful experiences?

Let's consider four practical ways:

• *Set an example.* If you, as teacher, simply and sincerely express your feelings of love and praise to God, you will encourage children to respond similarly. When you lead in prayer, pray spontaneously, briefly, in your natural speaking voice. Use child-size sentences and ideas. The child needs to understand that prayer is talking simply and honestly to God, his loving heavenly Father.

Share with the children your thoughts about God. Statements such as "God gave us a beautiful morning," "I love God," "I love the Lord Jesus," "God helps me every day—especially when I need to do hard things," "Let's thank God for ways He shows that He loves us," can help a child know that you as an adult recognize and rejoice in God's presence. Children may also begin to sense the reality of the Lord Jesus as they hear you talk about the Lord and talk to Him.

• *Give the child a chance to talk.* Sometimes our teaching/learning time is so filled with the teacher telling and the learner listening that children really do not have opportunities to ask questions, and to express their thoughts about and to God. Plan for a good balance of child talk and teacher talk. We sometimes say, "The children in my class just won't pray. They won't talk. They don't answer my questions."

Let's stop to consider this for a moment. Do they feel that you really want to listen to them? Do they know that what they say will be accepted? Do they have opportunities to ask questions as well as to respond to your questions? Children will talk! We need to give time to talk.

• *Listen! Really listen!* We have said to let children talk. But there is more. Be ready to listen, too. Show genuine interest in what they are saying. Many children live in a world in which no adult really listens to them. We can thoughtlessly interrupt children to say what we adults think is important.

When the early child arrives and begins to talk to us about what he feels is important, let us not be so hard at work preparing materials or getting ourselves ready to teach that we cannot take time to listen and share with a child. A listening adult can be a significant link in helping a child want to express his feelings and thoughts to a listening, caring God.

• *Provide small-group opportunities for prayer, praise and worship.* Often children will participate more readily in a small group rather than a large group. Encourage children to pray, express their love and praise during Bible Discovery time. Plan specific questions and comments you can use to guide the worship of children during this block of time in your program. For example, you might say, "Amy, I like the picture you've drawn of the mountains God has made. Let's tell God 'thank you' for the mountains."

CHECK YOURSELF

1. Consider the worship and fellowship experiences you are now providing for your children. According to the guidelines in this chapter do you think these experiences are meaningful for children? Why? Why not?

2. Identify how the sample Praise Time provided in this chapter gives children a meaningful worship and fellowship experience.

---

1. These materials are provided in "Living in God's Family," Gospel Light's churchtime curriculum kit for children.

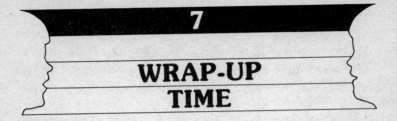

7

WRAP-UP TIME

What do you do with children in the churchtime session when the adult worship service runs longer than usual? There will be those times when you need to stretch the hour by 15 or 20 minutes. So you need some flexibility in the schedule.

Probably the most effective "flexing" can be done during the Wrap-Up Time by offering a variety of simple, Bible-related activities which children can do quietly in large or small groups, until dismissal time.

SAMPLE WRAP-UP TIME

Here's an example of how one church with about 25 children in the group planned the Wrap-Up Time at the conclusion of their session: At the end of Praise Time, the leader announced there would be four activities children could do until dismissal. The leader said, "Some of you may choose to work on a Bible game. Others can sit on the floor in the corner, listening to records. We also have some puzzles on the round table. And I know several of you want to look at the books on our bookshelf. This morning, the first grade girls can be the first to walk to the activity they want to do. Very good. Now the second grade girls can choose . . ." An adult stayed with each small group to converse with children until parents came for their children.

Other popular activities for Wrap-Up Time include: learning to play simple musical instruments such as an autoharp, melody or tone bells, or song flutes; viewing a filmstrip; planning an activity for next week; writing notes to absentees.

Occasionally, the leaders need to vary the Wrap-Up Time pattern. They can lead the children in large-group games that reinforce the day's learning while providing a relaxed, enjoyable conclusion to the session.

NOTE: Check your church library and Sunday School departments for available resources.

DISMISSAL TIME

Handling dismissal time so that everything flows smoothly is important. You will need to decide if children are to wait for parents to pick them up, or if children will be dismissed when the church service is over to find their parents on their own.

Here are some factors you will want to consider in making this decision: the ages of the children (Can the children be depended on to follow your instructions for meeting parents?); the size of your church facility (Can the children safely find their way around by themselves?); the location of your church (Is it near a busy street?), and your interest in building communication with parents. Having parents pick up their children allows weekly opportunity for you to greet them, and for them to see some of what goes on in your program.

With younger elementary-age children, it is best to extend the Wrap-Up Time period until parents have come for their children. Older children can usually be depended on to meet their parents as instructed.

IN CASE YOU'RE WONDERING . . .

1. How can we "stretch" Wrap-Up Time if the adult worship service runs longer than expected?

After 10 or 15 minutes of Wrap-Up Time, ask the children to move to other activities to prevent boredom. If the adult worship service continues even longer, play some of the games suggested for Get Together Time.

CHECK YOURSELF

1. List several activities which you could provide for Wrap-Up Time.

2. List several factors which will influence how you handle dismissal time.

3. List the major components of a churchtime schedule as discussed in this and the three preceding chapters. Describe the main focus of each.

PART III

MAKING
IT HAPPEN

8
WHAT ARE
THE TOOLS
WE NEED?

ROOM ENVIRONMENT

You hear people rave about restaurants with "lots of atmosphere." Architects and city planners worry about environmental impact. Why this interest in the appearance and impressions of people and places? Because what a place looks like and "feels" like are big factors in the success of any operation.

The church is no exception to this rule! Children (and adults) react both consciously and unconsciously to their surroundings. If a room is cheerful, clean and bright, children will feel like it is an important and happy place to be. If, on the other hand, a room is already in disorder or disrepair, children tend to add to the damage and will also take a more casual attitude toward what goes on there.

Any churchroom or building should be clean, well-kept and first rate in overall appearance. Then your children will assume that the church and its teachings are every bit as significant as the doctor's office, the school, and the shopping mall, which are usually kept clean and in repair. Places associated with God need to be taken care of equally as well.

How to Evaluate Your Room

You and your planning team can help create the right surroundings for the children in your program. The first step is to take a child's-eye view of the room in which you meet. One group of teachers did this by walking through their department on their knees. They were amazed at how many articles were out of sight or out of reach. Many small chores were difficult to handle. The result was some lowered shelves and tables and bulletin boards at the child's eye-level—all creating a room designed for children.

Try this same technique in your meeting place. Imagine you are a young child and note how the room impresses you. Does it make you feel warm and welcome? Is it cold and barnlike? Is it tiny and confining? Does it look like someone cares? Can you reach supplies and materials you'll need for learning activities?

Ways to Improve

On the basis of your evaluation, then, begin right away to adapt and improve your room environment. Be sure to work with Sunday School staff and others who use your room at other times so it will be suitable for all programs.

You don't need a lot of money to make a room cheerful and inviting. You can accomplish amazing things with color and ingenuity. Use attractive, lively colors; avoid beige and brown. Consider the size of your room when you choose colors; cool, light shades will give small rooms a spacious feeling. Oranges and yellows will make an oversized or drafty area seem warm and inviting. Lower bulletin boards to the eye-level of your children. Plants and window boxes can be donated by church members or purchased to add interest and color to your room.

Carpets and drapes are wonderful additions if you can obtain them, but are not absolutely essential to a good room environment. You can achieve nearly the same effect with cheery curtains and a large area rug or floor mats to sit on for activities. You might ask your ladies' group to sew these mats for you as a service project. But avoid loose pieces of carpeting which can become hazards as well as a floor maintenance problem.

Creating Usable Space[1]

What about solving the more complicated problems of limited space or awkward room design? Again, the key to success is not expense but ingenuity. If your room is crowded, start looking for "space wasters" you can eliminate. There may be tables, bookcases, filing cabinets, or excess chairs which have been there for so long no one has ever thought of moving them out. Do you use all the furniture in your room? Get rid of anything you don't use regularly. Is there a large walk-in closet or storage area that's big enough to transform for a discovery group? Can you make use of a nearby patio or other outdoor space? Can you trade rooms with a department that needs less space then you do?

An ideal arrangement will include several tables with

chairs around them (for Bible Discovery groups) and an assembly area with or without chairs (for Praise Time) (see sketch below).

OPEN ROOM ARRANGEMENT

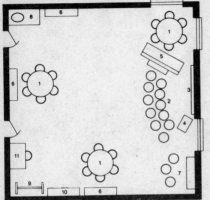

1. Table and chairs to seat 6–8 children for Bible Discovery Time.
2. Chairs (used at tables) grouped for Praise Time.
3. Bulletin board with picture rail.
4. Small table for leader's materials.
5. Piano (optional).
6. Low shelves for materials (glue, paper, crayons, etc.).
7. Bookshelf with several chairs.
8. Storage cabinets and sink counter.
9. Coatrack.
10. Shelves for take-home materials.
11. Secretary's desk.

Consider these alternatives as you plan.

1. Let children sit on the floor (on mats, if room is not carpeted) during Praise Time. This takes up less room than chairs and gives space for physical activity.

2. Use small classrooms with permanent walls for Bible Discovery Time and the assembly room for Praise Time.

3. If your room is small, before the large-group time begins, allow a few minutes for children to move their chairs and for leaders to move tables to edges of room.

4. Other ideas for using your space are illustrated in these sketches.

Turn the inside of a closet or cupboard into a study or reading corner.

Use the space on the back of piano or shelf units for displaying posters, art projects, etc.

Make a reading corner with shelf units, round rug and books.

One shelf unit used this way can create an area for a small discovery group.

5. If your room is too large for your program, strive for a cozy effect with color and floor coverings. Portable room dividers may be purchased or built (see sketch), and these will help close off an oversized area. These dividers also provide eye-level bulletin board space, and are ideal for use in a room where you are not free to put things on the wall.

SUPPLIES

Part of any good environment is an adequate supply of all the materials needed. You will need these items for your program:

Construction paper.

Inexpensive newsprint or note paper.

Crayons.

Pencils.

Felt markers.

Tempera paints, brushes, paint smocks.

Scissors.

Cellophane tape, masking tape.

Thumb tacks.

Glue, paste and/or gluesticks.

Shelf or butcher paper (rolled).

Paper towels.

Newspapers (for protecting tables and floors).

Paper cups, napkins or other supplies needed for refreshment time.

Clay or modeling dough.

If you do not have a sink in your room or easy access to one close by, you will need several plastic dishpans and pitchers, as well as sponges.

Be sure to plan ahead and check supplies well in advance of the day you want to use them!

To avoid confusion and prevent the problem of missing supplies, the best situation is to have your own cupboard or storage area at church for your supplies. If no storage space is available within your room, perhaps you can share storage space in a nearby room. Or, use a large briefcase, box or shopping bag and bring your supplies from home each week.

Some churches have designed a central supply room where all materials are kept. This system provides everyone with equipment and is a good arrangement when classroom storage space is limited.

Since you will probably be sharing a room used earlier by a Sunday School class, you may find it convenient to share a supply closet with the Sunday School staff. You can do this successfully if everyone is conscientious and cooperative. Labeled shelves or sections will identify each program's supplies. Discuss upcoming needs and projects with the person in charge of the Sunday School department involved. Be sure you agree on when and how supplies will be replenished, stored and maintained.

Another important aspect of the supply situation is audiovisual equipment. Spend some time with the person or church staff member in charge of these materials. Find out what equipment is available to you and how you can arrange to use it. Ask about record players, cassette recorders, slide and filmstrip projectors, screens, overhead projectors, and your church library of filmstrips and cassette tapes. (If you don't have a library, now might be a good time to start one!)

REMEMBER ...

With supplies and your meeting place all in good order, you can concentrate on meeting the needs of your children. Keep a sharp eye on your room, and always look for ways to improve your facilities. Do not leave "environmental impact" to the city planners. Remember its effect on your ministry to Christ's children! Roll up your sleeves; get out the paint brush and rally some capable volunteers. You can create a room that says, "Jesus Loves You" from wall to wall.

IN CASE YOU'RE WONDERING ...

1. What if I use a Sunday School room and have almost no time to set it up?

68

First of all, talk to the Sunday School staff coordinator to coordinate the transition between programs. Your Get Together Time materials should be portable (refreshments on a cart, game materials in a box), so these activities can begin as soon as churchtime people enter the room. Bible Discovery Time materials can be set out during Get Together Time but should be organized so no time is lost.

You might also consider the portable room dividers described in this chapter, along with portable easels, charts, chalkboards and bulletin boards. These things can be rolled into place quickly while children are playing games or having refreshments. Older children can help, and a room can be transformed in just a few minutes.

2. *What if I'm just not good at decorating?*

If you lack imagination where room improvements are concerned, look at catalogs, furniture advertisements and magazines for ideas. You will find helpful color and furniture arrangements that can be easily adapted. Most churches have at least one member who enjoys interior decorating and knows how to do it inexpensively. Get advice from him. Remember, improvements need not be expensive to be successful, but they do require planning and the desire to try something different.

3. *We have several grades together. Is it best to plan chairs for the comfort of the youngest or the oldest children?*

If you have only one size chair available, it is probably best not to have the older children sit on little chairs. Instead, use bigger chairs during Bible Discovery Time for all the children—but be sure to provide opportunity for movement to prevent restlessness in the younger children. If possible, remove the chairs completely and have the children sit on the floor for Praise Time.

4. How can we show films or filmstrips without blinds on the window?

Show films on the darkest wall of your room. If necessary, tape construction paper over windows nearest the screen or wall on which you project.

5. We have to combine several Sunday School departments into one churchtime group. What is the best use of facilities?

Coordinate this with the Sunday School staff. Hopefully, you will be able to choose the largest, most flexible and most easily accessible facilities for churchtime.

6. Our room is located so any loud noise is heard in the sanctuary. What can we do?

It seems that you have two choices: remind the children to sing and speak quietly, or move the children to a more remote room so that the spontaneity and activities of your program do not have to be minimized.

CHECK YOURSELF

1. List three or four reasons why room environment is an important aspect of your ministry.

2. Draw out a sketch of your present room arrangement. Then think of specific ways to improve your present room environment.

---

1. For more information, see the chapter on room environment in *Creative Bible Learning for Children: Grades 1–6,* by Barbara J. Bolton and Charles T. Smith.

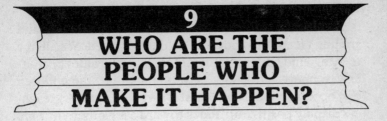

9
WHO ARE THE PEOPLE WHO MAKE IT HAPPEN?

LEADERSHIP QUALITIES

How would you describe someone who is effective in ministering to children? Your list of characteristics might vary somewhat from the order in which the qualities are listed below, but people with these qualities are usually your best choices for teachers. Seek to develop these qualities in yourself, and look for them as you recruit teachers, parent-helpers, and aides.

Loving. Love for children can be expressed in many different ways and by all personality types. A boisterous, laughing person and a soft-spoken, gentle person can be equally loving and caring. One major characteristic of those who genuinely love children is an awareness of children's needs. So the genuinely loving teacher will focus on ways to meet children's needs.

Positive. The influence of a cheerful personality and smiling face should never be underestimated. We all like to be around happy people. If teachers and aides encourage, support and gladly help one another, the children can observe models of Christ's love in action. As teachers display positive attitudes toward each other, they are building children's respect for others in the Body of Christ.

Friendly. Everyone needs a friend. And the children in your ministry will eagerly respond to a teacher who sincerely desires to be their friend. A friendly person is genuinely interested in others and takes time getting to know them. Asking questions, listening, sharing personal interests and hobbies all help to develop friendships with children.

Teachable. New and experienced teachers alike need periodic training opportunities. Although experience in working with children is not a prerequisite for churchtime teachers and aides, a desire to keep learning about children and discovering new ways of teaching effectively is an important attitude in any teacher. Even experienced people need to know what is expected of them in a particular situation. Give new teachers additional responsibility gradually as their understanding of children and effectiveness as a teacher grows.

STAFF REQUIREMENTS FOR YOUR PROGRAM

A simple rule-of-thumb for the number of teachers and aides you will need to help you is one teacher, parent-helper or aide for each 6-8 children. (See chap. 3 for suggestions on grouping children effectively.) Learning specialists agree that optimum learning takes place when the teacher/student ratio is maintained at this level.

JOB DESCRIPTIONS

Study this organizational chart and a description of the responsibilities for each of the staff members for a churchtime program. (NOTE: If you are in a large church, see Appendix E for additional helps.)

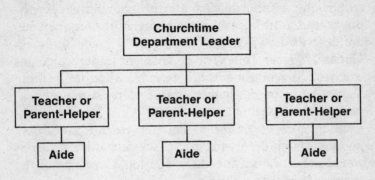

Churchtime Department Leader

The department leader guides and coordinates the teachers, parent-helpers and aides. He oversees and is responsible for the entire program and usually has a major part in the recruiting and training of the staff. He is able to suggest appropriate plans and materials, to encourage teachers, to recommend current resources and demonstrate methods.

The department leader is a listener. (Teachers need to know their suggestions and problems are being heard!) The leader is able to evaluate teaching skills and encourage teachers in areas of strength. Helping teachers to do their part also means the leader plans for and makes available the necessary equipment and materials.

The department leader is the chief communicator between the teachers, parent-helpers and aides in his department. The departmental leader is also concerned with establishing and maintaining communication with parents.

Times of planning, sharing and praying together as a staff are essential. Monthly (or more frequent) planning meetings are the responsibility of the department leader. (See the "PLANNING TOGETHER" section later in this chapter for specific suggestions.)

Specific responsibilities for the churchtime department leader during each time period of the program can be described as follows:

Get Together Time: The department leader welcomes each child while a teacher is responsible for leading games and a parent-helper or aide prepares the refreshments.

Bible Discovery Groups: The department leader may work with children with special needs and assist teachers in other ways as needed. He should lead one of the groups only if there are not enough teachers.

Praise Time: The department leader may lead the Praise Time each week and coordinates the involvement of other adults who assist with Praise Time.

Wrap-Up Time: The department leader makes sure that all games, books, records, and puzzles are available for use. The leader works with other teachers to guide and involve children in the planned activities. The department leader also greets parents and coordinates dismissal time.

Teacher

Here are specific responsibilities for teachers during each time period of the program.

Get Together Time: One teacher and a parent helper or aide may direct 15-20 minutes of games and refreshments. Games should be led by an enthusiastic person who can communicate clear directions to the group.

Bible Discovery Groups: Each teacher prepares, plans and directs a Discovery group activity. The teacher is responsible for gathering needed supplies for his group and for preparing aim-related questions and sentences to use in conversation with his group. Each group activity is usually repeated for four sessions during a unit, with a different group of children each session.

Praise Time: Each teacher participates in the Praise Time activities as planned by entire staff. Since the procedure of this time segment varies from week to week, the responsibilities of each teacher will also vary. For example, during a unit (usually four sessions), a teacher may tell the Bible story one week, participate in a puppet play, lead a memory verse game, or show a filmstrip another week.

Wrap-Up Time: Each teacher guides children in one of the activities provided during this time. Teachers supervise children until parents arrive.

Parent-Helper

Parent-helpers can provide significant expertise and assistance in various parts of the churchtime program. Utilize your parent-helpers for a unit's (four weeks) length of time according to their talents and interests. Many parent-helpers are capable of leading Get Together Time or Wrap-Up Time, of working with their own children to provide and serve refreshments, leading Bible Discovery groups, participating with their own children in puppet teams, or providing equipment and materials—like the puppet stage, costumes, choir robes, or curtains. Helping to decorate, arrange and maintain the room are also important responsibilities for parent-helpers who can serve during the week. (See chapter 10 for more details on parent involvement.)

Aide

Aides may be high school students, college-age or

other adults who work closely with the teachers. At the planning meeting for each unit, duties assigned to the aides may include serving and cleaning up refreshments, leading or assisting with Bible Discovery Time, directing games and music, or participating in other tasks as they are needed. Each aide's responsibilities will vary according to his interests and abilities.

Other Volunteers

A significant ministry can be provided by "specialist" volunteers. These are church members who can make special contributions to your children's program on a short-term basis.

Some people are excellent story tellers—use them as a special treat. People whose careers are of particular interest to children also make good "specialists"—such as Christian firemen, doctors, nurses, paramedics or policemen, missionaries, etc. The children will love having these people visit your group and tell something about their work.

People who are learning to live with handicaps such as deafness, blindness or paralysis and who have a positive witness to the Lord's help and who can handle children's quite direct questions might be interviewed and could speak briefly during Praise Time. Also, you might consider using craft, music, art or dramatic specialists for discovery groups that involve those activities.

RECRUITING HELPS

Now that you know what to look for, how do you recruit teachers, aides and volunteers? If recruiting is your responsibility, these helps will be profitable:

Pray for guidance. Ask God to provide you with key teachers who can do the job.

List prospective staff members. Consult with your pastor, director of Christian education or Sunday School superintendent before contacting any worker. Consider using older adults—like grandparents—in your program. These people make excellent aides and specialists because of their years of experience and accumulated knowledge. Many of them may be thrilled to work with children in the churchtime program. Also consider using single adults.

Use dependable, older high school and college-age aides. Try not to engage workers who are already teaching Sunday School and serving on several committees. Look for people who can make your program a priority in their schedules.

Contact prospective workers. Personally talk to each person on your list. Briefly describe the program to each person. Then say, "I've been praying for someone who can be a (leader, teacher, aide, parent-helper, specialist). I think you are capable, and would add much to the children's churchtime experiences. I would like you to consider accepting the responsibility for (this quarter)." State a specific time for which his help is needed. Ask him to think and pray about your request and then state a date by which you need his decision. Provide opportunities for each person to observe in the program and talk to you or others in the program if they have additional questions. Hopefully, you have a training program to which you can invite recruits.

Workers who are approached in this positive way realize the importance of the job. They need to know you have confidence in their abilities. And they need to know you are enthusiastic about the opportunities a churchtime program affords those who will guide children to know and grow in Christ.

Advertise your program. Make the congregation

aware of your program. Use your church bulletin, special flyers and posters and weekly church newsletter. Or prepare a special slide presentation to be shown to the whole congregation occasionally. Such publicity will keep people informed regarding what your program is accomplishing.

PLANNING TOGETHER

Everyone involved in your children's program needs to be a part of your planning team. Planning together is a priority item for a well-organized program. Teachers, aides, parent-helpers, and specialists all need to share ideas together and plan for effective teaching and learning.

As a result of planning together, staff members will have opportunity to learn from each other, pray together, and discover mutually agreeable solutions to problems. Teachers who plan together will be prepared and organized for their ministry.

Your planning team (consisting of all staff members) should meet prior to the beginning of each unit. Include these steps in your planning meeting.

1. Begin with prayer for your children and for each other. Ask God to help you find and use the most effective means possible to reach young lives.

2. Provide each of your staff with a copy of the Unit Plan Sheet (see p. 81). Discuss the theme of your unit, and the special projects and activities listed in your churchtime curriculum. (Everyone should read the unit before your meeting.) Decide which activities you will use, and who will be responsible for each phase of the unit. Ask everyone present to complete a Unit Plan Sheet to be sure everyone knows each person's assignment during each part of the session.

Begin by discussing the aims of the unit and deciding

78

how you will accomplish them through various parts of each session. Decide on specific responsibilities for each teacher, parent-helper and aide.

3. List supplies needed for the unit, and arrange to get anything not already available.

4. Become familiar with the songs in the unit by singing together the songs you will use with the children.

5. Allow a few minutes for problem solving, discussion of special needs, and evaluation of the previous unit.

IN CASE YOU'RE WONDERING ...

1. Is it a good idea to use high school age helpers?

Young people serving as aides can provide significant help in a churchtime program. They benefit by participating in and receiving excellent "on-the-job" training for ministry at the same time.

Coordinate your recruiting efforts with the youth leader so that you can use helpers who show spiritual maturity and leadership ability. Perhaps several teenagers could trade off duties or help on a short-term basis so that no young person consistently misses either Sunday School or the worship service. You might have a teenager work with the program for a full unit, then trade with another young person. Give a young person as much responsibility as he is able to handle. Be sure to include him as part of your planning team.

2. What if my staff is shorthanded due to illness or emergency?

Parent-helpers or specialists make good substitutes, especially if you can notify them early and help them plan activities.

If you are unaware of the problem until just prior to your program, first say to yourself, "I will not panic." Then rearrange your schedule or your groups to take care of the problem. For example, two Bible Discovery groups can be combined. Or you might choose one Discovery group activity for all children to work on.

Games or activities requiring much supervision can be replaced with familiar and less taxing activities. You can also use additional musical activities and extend portions of the Praise Time. If you can maintain a ratio of one teacher or aide for every 6-8 children, the shifting and "stop-gap" measures will be cut to a minimum.

3. I'm in a large church. How do I coordinate churchtime with the Sunday School?

That's an important question. See Appendix E for the answer to this question.

CHECK YOURSELF

1. Think of a Sunday School teacher or other adult who made a significant impact on your life. What was it about that person that impressed you? Then review the "Leadership Qualities" section of this chapter. Which qualities would you like to have God help you develop?

2. Review the responsibilities for the following people: Churchtime Department Leader, Teacher, Aide, Parent-Helper. Then diagram the organization needed for your churchtime program.

CHURCHTIME
UNIT PLAN SHEET

TITLE _____

DATES _____

UNIT AIMS
A description of what you want each child to know and be able to do after participating in a unit of Bible learning and Praise Time activities.

That each child _____

_____

_____

_____

_____

_____

STEP 1　　GET TOGETHER TIME (15–20 minutes)
A large group time of games and refreshments to meet physical and social needs of children.

	GAMES	REFRESHMENTS	PERSON(S) RESPONSIBLE
WEEK **1**			
WEEK **2**			
WEEK **3**			
WEEK **4**			

STEP 2　　BIBLE DISCOVERY TIME (20–30 minutes)
A small-group time of creative Bible learning experiences to meet intellectual, spiritual and social needs of children.

GROUP ACTIVITY	MATERIALS	PERSON(S) RESPONSIBLE

STEP 3   PRAISE TIME (20–30 minutes)

A large-group time of worship and fellowship experiences at a child's level to meet spiritual and social needs of children.

	LIST OF WORSHIP EXPERIENCES	PERSON(S) RESPONSIBLE
WEEK 1		
WEEK 2		
WEEK 3		
WEEK 4		

STEP 4   WRAP-UP TIME (5–15 minutes)

A large and/or small group time for children to use materials such as Bible games, records, puzzles and books to meet social and spiritual needs.

	ACTIVITIES	PERSON(S) RESPONSIBLE
WEEK 1		
WEEK 2		
WEEK 3		
WEEK 4		

10
LET'S MINISTER TO THE FAMILY

A child's family is where he first experiences love and where most of his early education takes place. During the elementary years, a child's family is of vital importance for his healthy development.

In your work with children, extending your ministry to their families is one of the most valuable efforts you can make.

Here are several ideas for ways you can minister to families.

KEEPING FAMILIES INFORMED

Regular communication with families of children who attend churchtime will help build good home-church relationships. Consider these possibilities for keeping your families informed:

• When your program is about to begin, have a meeting with parents of the children in your program. Introduce the leaders of the program; describe what will be happening; explain any special events you're planning; suggest ways that parents can participate; and so on.

• Have an "Open House" for your program at least annually. Display projects the children have made. Staff should be available to answer questions and give additional information on what the children are experiencing in your program. An "Open House" can be held at the conclusion of a session when the parents are arriving to pick up their children. Refreshments prepared by the children can be served.

• Send an "update" sheet home with the children once a quarter. Inform the parents about the theme of the unit; tell what the children will be doing; list parents who are participating; give information regarding any special events; and so on.

• Schedule a "Family Special" at least twice during the year. This could be a special family version of the regular churchtime program to which families of the children could be invited some evening. Provide Bible Discovery groups in which families can participate together. Include a time of sharing and singing, as well as simple refreshments, following your usual schedule.

INVOLVING THE PARENTS IN YOUR PROGRAM

Keeping your families informed is vital, but there are other important ways to involve parents in your program. Consider these possibilities:

• Ask parents to serve as volunteers for one unit (four weeks). Here are specific ways families can help:

Host Family: A family works together to prepare and serve refreshments during Get Together Time for one unit. Leader interviews one family member each week during Praise Time.

Resource Family: One or more families have a special skill which can be used for each Sunday of a unit in a Bible Discovery group, or in a special demonstration one Sunday in Praise Time. For example, one father or mother that has special artistic ability might draw a chalk picture of the Bible story as it is told during Praise Time. Another family with special musical abilities could lead a Bible Discovery group which is learning songs with motions and/or special rhythms.

You will find that many parents will serve when they know it will be for a limited period of time and will involve the use of skills they already have. Also, encourage parents to work together with their children on any of these activities.

• Involve parents in assisting with any special activities (outings, hikes, etc.) you schedule. There is always a need for transportation, refreshments, materials or help with supervision for these activities.

RELATING YOUR PROGRAM TO FAMILY CONCERNS

Another important way to extend your ministry to families is by relating the unit themes to family concerns. Helping children relate the Bible truths they are learning to family living will strengthen their relationships at home and be appreciated by parents.

Here are several specific ways to relate your program to family concerns:

• Encourage every leader in your program to become aware of concerns the children share regarding their families. Be good listeners as children mention the joys and challenges of life with their parents, brothers and sisters. In your personal conversation with the children, assure them that you care about what happens to them, and that God also cares about them.

• Build in references to family living during Bible

Discovery group time. Some themes in your curriculum will obviously relate quite easily to family life. As children work on their projects, guide them through conversation to think of ways their learning experiences can help them at home.

For example, as the children are working, you might ask, "When are times we may find it hard to show love at home?" "What is something you can share with your brothers or sisters?" "What is it about your father or mother for which you are especially thankful?" "What do you like to do with your family?"

• Build in references to family living in your Praise Time as well. Through the use of puppets, you can involve the children in thinking about family needs and concerns. For example, use puppets for acting out a family problem, such as sharing toys or showing love when you don't feel like it. Then involve children in discussing ways God can help them in family situations. By encouraging the children to relate their Bible learning to their everyday experiences at home, you will help tie what they are learning at church with their everyday family life.

• Occasionally, plan for one Bible Discovery Group to make "Family Living Kits" for the children to take home. For example, at Thanksgiving, Christmas or Easter time, have the children put together simple kits which their families could use for special Family Times at home. These kits could include a copy of *Family Life Today* magazine, as well as simple materials and instructions for a family worship time or family project. For instance, provide plans and materials for families to make place mats for a retirement home. Instruct the children on how to use the kits at home. At some later time, provide opportunity for the children to share their experiences in using these kits.

REMEMBER ...

The typical child spends a great deal of time at home, while he usually is involved in a church activity for only an hour or two a week. By extending your ministry to the families of the children, you can strengthen family relationships and help children relate their Bible learning to this significant area of their lives.

IN CASE YOU'RE WONDERING ...

1. How can I help the child who comes from a single parent home, foster home or who lives in a home for children?

Your attitude toward children in these particular situations will be very important. Be sure they don't feel excluded or less important because their family situation is different from other children. Emphasize that all our families are different from each other. Some have grandparents, and brothers or sisters, while others don't.

Prior to announcing a family activity, talk to the child and let him know what other "special" arrangement can be made. You may have another family in the program take a special interest in the child who lives separated from his father; and vice versa for the child whose mother is not present in the home. Remember to let each child know that he is special in his or her own way, and that God's love can be experienced by all people, no matter what their families are like.

2. I'm a busy person. About all I can do is get ready for the children's program. Is it really essential to reach out to the families of the children?

Yes, it really is important. But there are many ways to show concern to families which do not take a great deal of time. A postcard or phone call shows a family that you care if you are aware of a special need they have. Speaking briefly to parents at the beginning or conclusion of each session is a simple way of ministering to families.

Coordinating your efforts with the Sunday School staff will also help you make the best use of your time. Remember your purpose is not just to run a program one hour a week. Your goal is to influence children's growth beyond your weekly children's program.

CHECK YOURSELF

1. Review ways of informing parents about your program. What would be the best ways for your situation?

2. List four ways for parents to be involved in and help with your program.

3. List three areas of family living which you can relate to themes of the program.

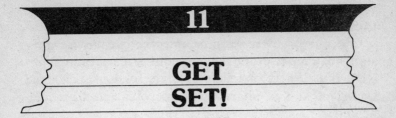

11

GET
SET!

TRAINING IDEAS

The next step in preparing for your extended program with children is the training of teachers, parent-helpers, and aides. Without training, the effectiveness of your workers will be greatly diminished. Teachers and aides who know their tasks, the purpose of these tasks and have begun to learn the skills required to accomplish these tasks will be more likely to succeed in guiding Bible learning experiences for children. (NOTE: the person responsible for the training of Christian education workers in your church especially needs to be aware of the ideas provided in this chapter.)

This chapter provides material for a two-hour training session (or two one-hour sessions) as well as some specific suggestions for introducing aides and parent-helpers into your program. Before you plan for these training sessions, recruit your staff (including aides) using the guidelines and helps in chapter 9.

Plan to use these sessions on two consecutive nights, one night a week for two consecutive weeks, or in Saturday sessions. Prior to the training sessions, distribute copies of this handbook to all teachers and aides.

1. Let's Get Acquainted (10 minutes)

Welcome everyone to the session. Ask the people to introduce themselves to one another by sharing information about themselves and their families. Begin with prayer. Lead a brief discussion based on chapter 1, "Let's Begin with the Basics." Ask participants to read these Bible verses: 1 Timothy 4:10,11; 1 Peter 5:2,3; 1 Timothy 4:12 and 1 John 3:16. After you have discussed these qualities of a teacher, divide participants into groups of three to share responses to this question: "Which of these is the easiest for you to do? The hardest? Why?"

2. Ministry Goals (20 minutes)

Before this training session, ask one person to read and briefly summarize chapter 2. As you discuss together the goals listed in chapter 2, use these questions as a guide: "What other goals would you add to this list? Which of these goals is the most important to you?"

3. Programming (20 minutes)

Before this training session, ask several people to be ready to briefly describe each time period in the program listed in chapters 4—7. After they share, discuss each of these time periods. Then use this matching game as a way of reinforcing the aims and activities of each period in the program. Letter 8½x11-inch (21.5x27.5-cm) sheets of paper as in sketch. Distribute cards to participants. Have each person—one at a time—with name of time period hold up his card. The person with matching card then reads the correct description of this part of the churchtime program. Continue until all four segments of the program have been correctly identified and described.

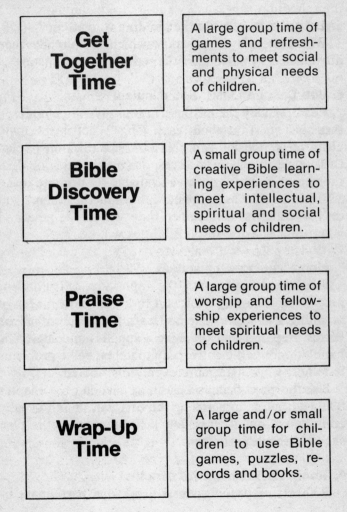

Get Together Time	A large group time of games and refreshments to meet social and physical needs of children.
Bible Discovery Time	A small group time of creative Bible learning experiences to meet intellectual, spiritual and social needs of children.
Praise Time	A large group time of worship and fellowship experiences to meet spiritual needs of children.
Wrap-Up Time	A large and/or small group time for children to use Bible games, puzzles, records and books.

4. Schedule (10-15 minutes)

As a group look at the schedules in chapter 3 of this book. Discuss each schedule option and evaluate together which schedule would best fit with your church situation. Use these questions as a guide. "How long a time period does our program need to be? In adapting the schedules suggested, what are we planning to do to meet the basic needs of the children who attend?" (OPTION: Describe the schedule which has already been determined by your Christian education leadership.)

5. Job Descriptions (10-15 minutes)

Read through the job descriptions given in chapter 9. Ask this question about each job, "What is the main purpose/responsibility of this job?" Use this time to plan and/or clarify who will be responsible for each job. List the parent-helpers you have available (or begin to make a list and make assignments for contacting them) and decide which staff member they will be helping and what their specific responsibilities will be.

6. Unit Planning (30 minutes)

Emphasize to the group the importance of team planning for each unit. Ask group to list the advantages of planning together as a team (learn from each other, be better prepared and organized, supplies and materials handled more efficiently, pray together, solve problems together, work load more evenly distributed, etc.).

Use the plan sheet and planning agenda from chapter 9 as your guide to planning the first unit (a unit usually consists of four weeks). Duplicate a copy of the plan sheet for each participant.

7. Room Environment (20 minutes)

Before this training session, ask one participant to

read chapter 8. Ask this person to briefly summarize some guidelines for room environment. Then, guide the group to evaluate the room you will be using according to these guidelines. Ask, "What does this room tell children about God? What changes do we need to make?" You may need to plan and work with the Sunday School staff or others who also use the room.

Conclude the training session by praying together about the specific responsibilities you all will have.

TRAINING PARENT-HELPERS AND AIDES

Step 1: Once you have recruited parent-helpers and aides, arrange for a time to give them a brief overview of the program and its schedule. If possible have these people observe your program in action. Tell them to specifically observe the person whose job is similar to what they will be doing.

Step 2: Each aide and volunteer should clearly understand what will be expected of him or her. Listing responsibilities on paper is often helpful for aides and volunteers. Make sure each person understands what materials he is expected to bring, and where supplies are located at church. Be sure to include parent-helpers and aides in your monthly planning meeting.

Step 3: After the aide or volunteer has successfully completed his service, ask him these questions as a means of evaluation, "What did you especially enjoy about working with us in churchtime? What was hard for you? Did you have the materials you needed? When will you be able to help us again?"

PROMOTIONAL IDEAS

Consider using some or all of the following ideas as a means of publicizing your churchtime program to children and their parents.

93

1. Place a weekly announcement in your church bulletin or church newsletter.

2. Announce the program in children's Sunday School classes with a brief invitation and description of activities.

3. Announce the program in the adult Sunday School classes so parents will be informed about your plans.

4. Distribute flyers/letters to parents and children.

5. Make posters to be displayed at the church advertising the program.

IN CASE YOU'RE WONDERING ...

1. If I'm the only leader, or if there are just two of us, will this training program still work?

It is best, if at all possible, to work through these training ideas with another person. Until you find additional help, read through this book and complete the Check Yourself section at the end of each chapter.

2. How can these training ideas be combined with our ongoing training program for children's workers?

If you have an annual or continuing training program, schedule your churchtime training at the same time. Have all participants meet together for general information and instructions. You may want to schedule some time together for coordinating use of rooms, materials, schedules, etc., as well as discussing topics of mutual interest (such as guided conversation, leading a child to Christ, music, and discipline).

Then divide into sections, grouping participants according to the program they are involved with (i.e., Sunday School departments, churchtime, weekday, etc.).

3. What are some other ways to get new ideas and improve our children's program?

There are many other training programs for leaders

and aides to attend. Children's division seminars and clinics sponsored by the International Center for Learning are excellent opportunities for further training. Write P.O. Box 1650, Glendale, California, 91209 for information.

I..C.L. also has four age-level training kits available. These *Creative Christian Education Resources* kits include posters, transparencies, filmstrips, cassettes and a leader's guide for use in training your Christian education staff.

Sunday School conventions and workshops may also be a source of additional resources and training. Use books and resources as a means of discovering new methods and ideas. (See chapter 12 for suggestions.) Occasionally you may want to observe other churches' programs for children for ideas you can use.

CHECK YOURSELF

1. List three reasons why a training program is essential for leaders of children's programs.

2. List three steps for training parent-helpers.

3. What are three or four ways you would effectively publicize your children's program to both children and adults in your church?

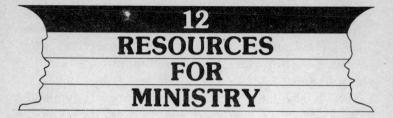

12
RESOURCES FOR MINISTRY

BOOKS FOR TEACHERS AND LEADERS

Bolton, Barbara J., and Charles T. Smith. *Creative Bible Learning for Children: Grades 1—6.* Glendale, CA: Regal Books, 1977. Basic for a children's ministry.

_____. *Bible Learning Activities: Children, Grades 1—6.* Glendale, CA: Regal Books, 1973.

Canfield, Jack, and Wells, Harold C. *100 Ways to Enhance Self-Concept in the Classroom.* Englewood Cliffs, NJ: Prentice-Hall, 1976.[1]

Cressy, Byron. *Discipline and Children.* Glendale, CA: ICL Concept Book, G/L Publications, 1977. Guidelines on discipline for teachers and parents.

Getz, Jana. *Merry Voices: Happy Songs.* Wheaton, IL: Tyndale House Publishers, 1976.

Haystead, Wesley. *You Can't Begin Too Soon.* Glendale, CA: Regal Books, 1974. Guidelines for introducing young children to God.

Heermann, Keith. *Outreach to Children.* Glendale, CA: ICL Concept Book, G/L Publications, 1978. An outreach strategy for children's ministry.

Larson, Jim, ed. *Make Learning a Joy.* Glendale, CA: Regal Books, 1975. Making children's Bible learning meaningful.

LeBar, Mary E. *Children Can Worship.* Wheaton, Illinois: Victor Books, 1976.

Rottman, Fran. *Easy-to-Make Puppets and How to Use Them: Children/Youth.* Glendale, CA: Regal Books, 1978.

Rowen, Dolores. *Easy-to-Make Crafts for Children Ages 3 to 11.* Glendale, CA: Regal Books, 1976.

_____. *Easy-to-Make Crafts for Preteens and Youth.* Glendale, CA: Regal Books, 1976.

Sample, Mabel S. *Music-Making with Older Children.* Nashville: Convention Press, 1972.

Schorr, Vernie. *Building Relationships with Children.* Glendale, CA: ICL Concept Books, G/L Publications, 1978.

Smith, Barbara, and Smith, Charles. *Non-Musician's Guide to Children's Music.* Glendale, CA: ICL Concept Book, G/L Publications, 1977.

RESOURCES FOR TEACHERS AND CHILDREN

Alexander, David S. *The New Testament in Living Pictures; The Old Testament in Living Pictures.* Glendale, CA: Regal Books, 1972. Pictures of Bible lands.

Arch Books. St. Louis, MO: Concordia. A collection of Bible stories for young readers.

Barrett, Ethel. Christian Values Tales *Buzz Bee; Quacky* and *Wacky; Gregory Grub; Blister Lamb.* Glendale, CA: Regal Books, 1978. Book/cassette series on Christian values.

_____. *Ethel Barrett Tells Bible Stories to Children,* Vols. 1 and 2. Glendale, CA: Regal Books, 1977.

_____. *Ethel Barrett Tells Favorite Bible Stories.* Glendale, CA: Regal Books, 1978.

Beers, Gilbert. *God Is My Helper; God Is My Friend; Jesus Is My Teacher; Jesus Is My Guide.* Grand Rapids, MI: Zondervan, 1973.

Bible Story Pop-Up Books. *Jesus Calms the Storm; Jonah; Three in a Furnace.* Glendale, CA: Regal Books, 1978.

Braga, Meg. Riddle Rhyme Fun Books: *What Do You Hear?; What Helps?; What Is Inside?; What Do You See?* Glendale, CA: Regal Books, 1977. "Finish me" books for children.

Diamond, Sylvia. *The Good Shepherd; Hidden Treasure.* Glendale, CA: Regal Books, 1977.

Fergus, Meryl. *Discovering at the Zoo; Discovering Colors; Discovering Little Things; Discovering Out of Doors.* Glendale, CA: Regal Books, 1974.

"God's Wonderful World" series. Glendale, CA: Regal Books, 1978. Doodle art makes reading fun.

How-to-Use Your Bible Cards, Pacs 1,2,3,4. Glendale, CA: G/L Publications, 1973. Helpful for developing Bible study skills.

Luke Street Books. *The Country House; Peter's House; The Crowded House; The Special House; The Guest House; The Rich House; The Cheat's House; The Little Girl's House.* Glendale, CA: Regal Books, 1978.

My Bible Story Activity Coloring Books, Books 1,2,3. Glendale, CA: Regal Books, 1977. Bible story activities.

Pointing-Out Books. *God's Friends; Meet Jesus.* Glendale, CA: Regal Books, 1977.

Ranger Rick Magazine. Excellent children's magazine on nature and conservation. Address: National Wildlife Federation, 1412 16th St. NW, Washington, DC 20036.[1]

Wonders of Creation. Glendale, CA: Regal Books, 1975. Beautiful pictures of God's creation.

World Magazine. Colorful children's nature magazine. Address: National Geographic World, Dept. 00977, 17th and M St., Washington, DC 00977.[1]

Booklets—Gospel Light Publications. *God Wants You to Be a Member of His Family; God Wants You to Know How to Live as His Child; God Wants You to Talk with Him About Everything; God Wants You to Know He Cares About You.*

FILMS, RECORDS AND OTHER LEARNING RESOURCES

Choose audiovisual resources and children's books from the sources listed below. Request a current catalog from which to make appropriate selections:

Ken Anderson Films, P.O. Box 618, Winona Lake, IN 46590.

John T. Benson Publishing Company (and Impact Records), 1625 Broadway, Nashville, TN 37202.

Broadman Press, 127 Ninth Street, Nashville, TN 37234.

Concordia, 3558 S. Jefferson Ave., St. Louis, MO 63118.

Family Films, 14622 Lanark Street, Panorama City, CA 91420.

International Center for Learning, 110 W. Broadway, Glendale, CA 91204. Training resources.

North American Liturgy Resources, 2110 W. Peoria Ave., Phoenix, AZ 85029.

Paragon, 803 18th Ave., Nashville, TN 37203.

Puppet Productions, P.O. Box 82008, San Diego, CA 92138.

Teleketics, 1-39 S. Santee Street, Los Angeles, CA 90015.

Word, Inc., Box 1790, Waco, TX 76703.

NOTE: Always preview films and filmstrips before

use with children to plan discussion ideas and to be certain the resources are appropriate to the interests and understanding of the viewers.

FAMILY LIFE RESOURCES

Briggs, Dorothy Corkille. *Your Child's Self-Esteem.* New York: Doubleday, 1970.[1]

Dobson, James. *Dare to Discipline.* Wheaton, IL: Tyndale House Publishing, 1970.

_____. Family Life Booklets: *Love, Anger, Guilt,* and *God's Will.* Glendale, CA: G/L Publications, 1976.

_____. *Hide or Seek.* Old Tappan, NJ: Fleming H. Revell Company, 1974.

Dreikurs, Rudolph. *Children: The Challenge.* New York: Hawthorn Book Co., 1964.[1]

Family Life Today magazine. Glendale, CA: G/L Publications.

Foster, Timothy. *Dare to Lead.* Glendale, CA: G/L Publications, 1977.

Gordon, Thomas. *Parent Effectiveness Training.* New York: Peter H. Wyden, 1973.[1]

Rickerson, Wayne. *Good Times for Your Family.* Glendale, CA: G/L Publications, 1977.

Satir, Virginia. *Peoplemaking.* Palo Alto, CA: Science and Behavior Books, 1972.[1]

Wakefield, Norm. *You Can Have a Happier Family.* Glendale, CA: G/L Publications, 1977.

Walker, Georgiana, ed. *The Celebration Book.* Glendale, CA: G/L Publications, 1977.

---

1. These resources listed are not written in a Christian context but are included because of their practical, basic information for leaders, teachers and parents of children.

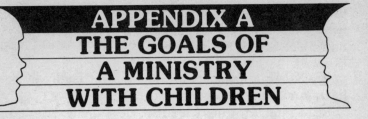

APPENDIX A
THE GOALS OF
A MINISTRY
WITH CHILDREN

(NOTE: This Appendix is provided as additional resource for anyone responsible for planning an overall ministry to children.)

Have you ever heard a statement such as this before? "If you don't know where you're going, you'll never know for sure if you got there!"

As you make your plans for ministry to children, you need to think together about what you are really trying to accomplish. What do you want children to experience as a result of their involvement in the Christian education ministry of your church? What do you hope elementary-age children will learn in the church?

Defining your ministry goals is the first step in developing a vital and interesting program for children. Well-defined goals to which you are committed become points of reference for deciding questions about program, approach, schedule, etc. Let's consider several important goals for a church's *Christian education ministry with children.* Each child needs to:

KNOW God loves him and sent His Son Jesus Christ to be his Saviour;

BECOME a member of God's forever family by believing in Jesus as Saviour and Lord;

BE a vital, growing Christian, developing a style of living which is pleasing to God and which shows others he is a believer in and follower of Jesus Christ;

DEVELOP a personal, growing relationship with God, seeking His guidance in all life's problems;

LOVE and VALUE the Bible, God's Word;

LEARN SKILLS for personal Bible study, so that the child can discover for himself what God's Word means to him;

ENJOY the church, Christ's Body, as a group of people who can help him worship the Lord God;

DEVELOP Christian friendships;

IDENTIFY his God-given talents so he can develop and use them for God's glory;

SERVE AND LOVE others by finding opportunities to help and share his faith with others.

Plan to meet with other teachers and leaders involved with the children's ministry of your church. List together the programs in your church's ministry. Then discuss how the overall goals just described are (or are not) being implemented in your church's ministry to children.

When a child comes to church, he does not leave everything but his spiritual concerns at home; he arrives with all of his needs and concerns. Thus, a Christian education program should be designed to meet physical, emotional, social and spiritual needs. What an opportunity to help the child understand that God is sufficient for every need he has!

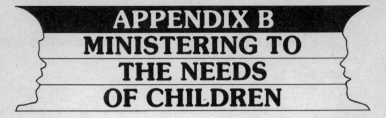

APPENDIX B
MINISTERING TO
THE NEEDS
OF CHILDREN

Your calling as a teacher of children involves you in a ministry to the whole child—with all of his physical, emotional, spiritual, social and intellectual needs. The importance of close relationships with each of your children becomes obvious if you are to gear Bible truths to specific needs children have.

In one sense, you are a "detective" as you teach. Look for clues that will identify areas of interest and need for each child. Devising a simple chart can help you gear your teaching in this direction. Put the names of all of your children on a chart such as the one shown below, or have one page per child. Fill in pertinent information as you become aware of it through observation and conversation: Does the child come from a happy home? Does he feel good about himself? What problems bother him? Consult with the child's Sunday School teachers and parents so that you have insights from several people who work with that child.

NEEDS CHART

NEEDS	CHILD 1	CHILD 2	CHILD 3
SPIRITUAL What is his understanding of what it means to be a member of God's family?			
SOCIAL Shy? Aggressive? Needs attention? Needs more freedom? Needs more structure?			
EDUCATIONAL Learns quickly? Learns slowly?			
SPECIAL INTERESTS Hobbies? Skills? Talents? Enjoys most?			
FAMILY BACKGROUND Father? Mother? Brothers and/or sisters?			
SPECIAL NEEDS Feels good about himself? Any problems that bother him?			

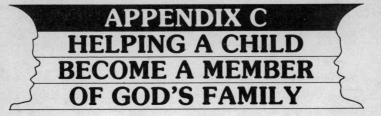

APPENDIX C
HELPING A CHILD
BECOME A MEMBER
OF GOD'S FAMILY

The age at which a child grasps the meaning of personal salvation is greatly influenced by his training and background. Salvation is a supernatural work of the Holy Spirit. Unless the Spirit is working in the child's heart and mind, he cannot become a child of God. Therefore, begin by praying for wisdom and sensitivity in seeking to deal with every child's spiritual needs.

Since children are easily influenced to follow a group, avoid group appeals. Plan for personal conversation and prayer with a child who appears responsive.[1]

The following conversation took place as a teacher named Mrs. Hilton talked with a boy named Warner about God's love.

Mrs. Hilton: Warner, why do you think God wants you in His family?

Warner: I dunno.

Mrs. Hilton: Because He loves you very much. Read what God's Word says about that here in 1 John.

Warner: "God is love" (1 John 4:8).

Mrs. Hilton: But Warner, you and I and everyone in the world don't deserve God's love because we all have done wrong things. The Bible's word for doing wrong is sin. Read what God's Word says about our sin.

Warner: "All have sinned and fall short of the glory of God" (Romans 3:23).

Mrs. Hilton: What do you think should happen to us because we sin—because we do wrong things?

Warner: I guess we should be punished.

Mrs. Hilton: That's right, Warner. But God still loves you and me so much that He sent Jesus Christ to take the punishment we should get for our sin. Do you know how Jesus took our punishment?

Warner: He died on the cross?

Mrs. Hilton: Yes, Warner, He did. Tell me how you feel about the wrong things you have done.

Warner: I don't know. (pause) I don't like them, I guess.

Mrs. Hilton: Can you say that to God right now?

Warner: OK .... I'm sorry, God. I've done lots of wrong things. And I wish I hadn't. Amen.

Mrs. Hilton: And how do you feel about Jesus loving you so much that He took your punishment and died for you?

Warner: Kind of sad, I guess. But sort of glad, too.

Mrs. Hilton: What part makes you glad?

Warner: I'm glad Jesus loves me enough to do that.

Mrs. Hilton: Can you tell God that, too?

Warner: Dear God. I know you love me and that Jesus died for me. Thank you ... thanks a lot.

Mrs. Hilton: Warner, if you really are sorry for your

sins and if you believe Jesus died for you, God says that He forgives all your sin. And do you know what happens when God forgives you?

Warner: No.

Mrs. Hilton: He makes you His child, part of His forever family. Read this verse and tell me what it says about you.

Warner: "As many as received Him, to them He gave the right to become the children of God" (John 1:12, *NASB*). That means I'm a child of God—I'm in His family!

---

1. An attractive booklet titled, *God Wants You to Be a Member of His Family* presents the plan of salvation in children's language and is available from your church supplier.

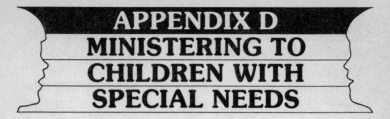

APPENDIX D
MINISTERING TO CHILDREN WITH SPECIAL NEEDS

1. How do I handle the hyperactive child?

A clinically hyperactive child is different from a child who can't sit still for very long. The hyperactive child reacts to life the way you would respond to being closed in a room with the television, radio, stereo system, and two vacuum cleaners all turned up full blast. Sound like too much for you? A classroom often seems like "too much" for the hyperactive child.

Hyperactive children are unable to concentrate on one thing at a time. They are in constant motion mentally, and often physically as well. Since such a child is unable to sit and listen or even to work on one project for any length of time, he leaps from one distraction to another, and often distracts others at the same time.

In your ministry with children, hyperactive children need your special love and patience. Such children also need more adult guidance and attention, so plan for additional staff.

Be sure that hyperactive children are involved primarily in quiet activities which help them keep their energies channeled rather than in activities which accentuate hyperactivity. Hyperactive children function best with a minimum of distraction and an activity which captures their attention.

As you show love to hyperactive children, be aware of the needs of the other children in your program at the same time. If your program is to have maximum effectiveness, you cannot allow one or a few children to distract others unnecessarily or reduce your program to chaos.

A hyperactive child may need individual attention from a teacher or a leader of your program. Consultation with parents as to the most effective ways to handle his hyperactivity can also be beneficial.

2. *How do I handle shy children?*

A shy child often feels insecure and afraid. It is important that such a child feel secure and loved. Encourage the children in your program to help others feel welcome and important. This will happen as the leaders do it and teach by their good example.

Do not push a shy child to talk in a large group. A rather quiet child will usually feel more free to talk in a small group in which every child is freely participating. Such a child may eventually feel free to speak up in a large group after he has had successful experiences in smaller groups.

3. *What about the aggressive child?*

Again, the rule is to accept each child as he is. Every time there is positive behavior be sure that a child knows that you appreciate his efforts.

Your good example of showing love to others by encouraging and affirming them will also be helpful in teaching children how to relate to each other.

At the same time, you need to be concerned with the welfare of all children. If a child is being aggressive enough to upset or harm another child, you will need to be firm but positive, remove the aggressive child from the situation, and clearly explain the behavior necessary in order to return.

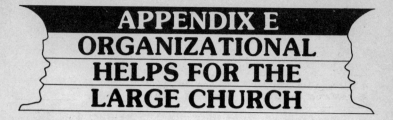

APPENDIX E
ORGANIZATIONAL HELPS FOR THE LARGE CHURCH

Organizational Chart

An effective children's ministry in a large church can take place when all of the programs are carefully coordinated. Study the organizational chart on the following page.

Note the addition of a children's division coordinator for the Children's Division. A children's division coordinator is essential whenever there are four or more departments within grades one through six in Sunday School or churchtime.

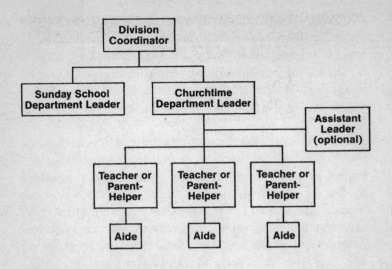

Job Description for the
Children's Division Coordinator

This person is responsible to the general superintendent or the director of Christian education. The division coordinator is an experienced teacher and leader who supervises and directs the work of the entire children's division of the Sunday School and churchtime, grades one through six. He insures that the ministries of Sunday School and churchtime complement and support each other.

Within the Christian education policy for recruitment the division coordinator seeks out, trains and organizes personnel for the entire division. He consistently makes available opportunities for training prospective staff members for each department. The coordinator also assists department leaders in preparing for their monthly or weekly departmental planning meetings.

Since the coordinator is directly responsible to the general superintendent or director of Christian education, he must be the communication link between the

Christian education board (committee, etc.) and the department leaders of Sunday School and churchtime. At regularly scheduled meetings with department leaders he shares information vital to the smooth running of all programs. He coordinates the use of supplies, equipment and facilities for programs in the children's division.

The division coordinator is continually envisioning the space and equipment necessary for growth. He makes recommendations to the general superintendent to develop and maintain departments and classes of the proper size and to control the teacher-student ratio by creating new departments and classes. Planning regularly with department leaders is vital to insure cooperation and facilitate an orderly and consistent growth.

Regular, firsthand observation of each department is essential for evaluation purposes. (Alerting department leaders ahead of time prevents their being surprised.) The coordinator shares the evaluation personally with each department leader, pointing out strengths as well as opportunities for improvement.